Buying
Real Estate
Foreclosures

Buying Real Estate Foreclosures

Third Edition

Melissa Kollen-Rice

McGraw-Hill

New York   Chicago   San Francisco   Lisbon   London   Madrid
Mexico City   Milan   New Delhi   San Juan   Seoul
Singapore   Sydney   Toronto

The *McGraw·Hill* Companies

1 2 3 4 5 6 7 8 9 0   FGR/FGR   0 1 4 3 2 1 0 9 8

ISBN 978-0-07-154661-4

MHID   0-07-154661-8

This publication is designed to provide accurate and authoritative informa-tion in regard to the subject matter covered. It is sold with the understand-ing that neither the author nor the publisher is engaged in rendering legal, accounting, futures/securities trading, or other professional service. If legal advice or other expert assistance is required, the services of a competent professional person should be sought.

—From a Declaration of Principles jointly adopted
by a Committee of the American Bar Association
and a Committee of Publishers

McGraw-Hill books are available at special quantity discounts to use as premiums and sales promotions, or for use in corporate training programs. To contact a representative, please visit the Contact Us pages at www.mhprofessional.com.

For Steve—my best friend, my inspiration, my knight in shining armor, and the love of my life

For Jimmy—my pride and joy, my rising superstar, and the wealth of my life

For Mom—my "momager," my heart and soul, the wind beneath my wings, and the angel in my life

For Tom and Maggie—my guiding lights of love, support, wisdom, and kindness—and the glow in my life

Contents

Table of Sample Forms, Illustrations, and Checklists

Preface

In the first edition of *Buying Real Estate Foreclosures* (1991), I introduced readers to the foreclosure market with this innovative step-by-step guidebook that included practical, street-smart techniques for beginners and experienced foreclosure purchasers based on my 10 years of experience in buying, selling, renting, and creatively financing hundreds of real estate properties.

In the second edition of *Buying Real Estate Foreclosures* (2003), I expanded the best-selling guidebook with reader-friendly features, including introductions and summaries for each chapter to help readers focus on each stage of the foreclosure purchasing procedure, Internet Web sites to help readers locate the most up-to-date sources of foreclosure listings, and helpful tips for financing foreclosures.

In this third edition of *Buying Real Estate Foreclosures* (2008), drawing on my legal experience, I have updated the guidebook once again to reflect the latest developments in the foreclosure marketplace and to help readers uncover, and benefit from, today's newest foreclosure opportunities *safely* and *sanely*, while avoiding potential risks. In addition to the unique features, comprehensive checklists, and step-by-step purchasing techniques that have set this book apart from any others on this topic, this expanded revision also includes

- Ways to benefit from the Mortgage Debt Cancellation Relief Act, and other recent groundbreaking foreclosure legislation on both state and national levels, and the essential steps that readers must take in order to comply with these new laws

- Strategies and checklists for negotiating "short sales" with sellers and the foreclosing lenders
- A guide for calculating your foreclosure purchasing budget
- Tips for raising your FICO score
- The latest financing strategies (that won't come back to haunt you)
- More "due diligence" questions to ask—and investigate—before you buy a foreclosure
- More safety tips that can save your life
- A state-by-state foreclosure fact sheet
- A comprehensive new glossary of foreclosure terms

Melissa S. Kollen-Rice

Acknowledgments

I gratefully acknowledge the following people for their invaluable contributions to the third edition of *Buying Real Estate Foreclosures*.

My Family

To **Steve**, for being my hero, preserving my sanity, for loving me so flawlessly, and for treating me "like a diamond" every day of my life. Your unselfish support, sacrifice, and faith in me are the foundation of my happiness, and your love is the driving force behind everything I accomplish.

To **Jimmy**, for having the courage and drive to achieve excellence— thank you for understanding and supporting my dream and for being the best son any parent could hope for. From the moment you were born, it has been, is, and will always be my privilege to be your mother.

To **Mom**, for being my manager, my lifelong role model, and my brave angel. Thank you for bringing me up in an environment that values advocacy and compassion.

To **Jack**, for letting me "adopt" you and for being such an honorable, beloved addition to our family.

To **Tom** and **Maggie**, for your love and support, proof that you don't have to be blood-related to be "family."

To **Matt** and **Beth**, and **Lindsey** and **Kim**, **Laura** and **Bob**, **Sharlene**, **George**, and **Sharlet**, for being so patient and supportive in arranging holidays and birthdays around my crazy schedule and for forgiving my absences so graciously.

My Literary Support System

Jake Elwell, my literary agent; for tirelessly promoting this revision and making this happen.

Mary Glenn, editorial director for McGraw-Hill, for being on my team, supporting my ideas, and seamlessly guiding this book through to production.

Ed Chupak, editorial coordinator for McGraw-Hill, for your patience, encouragement, and technical assistance in the production of this third edition.

Ruth Mannino, Senior Production Supervisor for McGraw-Hill, for your dedication to this project, for keeping everything on schedule, and for making this the best edition yet.

Alice Manning, copyeditor, for your incredible talent in finding the right words and putting them where and how they belong.

Introduction

How many of you have bosses who stay up late at night thinking of ways to help you make a lot of money? On the other hand, how many of you have worked diligently for others, for many years, and have made them a lot of money? You will never get ahead by waiting for a boss to give you what you think you deserve. You have to take control of your own destiny.

Whether you are a renter who is in pursuit of the "American dream of home ownership" or an investor who is looking to build wealth, *Buying Real Estate Foreclosures* will help you to achieve your goal, safely and sanely. By choosing real estate in general, and foreclosures in particular as your vehicle to success, you have joined thousands of entrepreneurs who started out along the same path as you are now— with a dream and the motivation to attain it.

The vast majority of people use their money to buy furniture, furs, jewelry, and other luxury items. But in five years, will a $5000 living room set be worth more, or less? The answer, of course, is less. Entrepreneurs are different. We want more. We will forgo immediate gratification for future gain, and we look to buy things like real estate, which will be worth more in five years.

Now, I am not going to tell you that buying foreclosures is a "get rich quick" endeavor. With few exceptions, everything that is rewarding in life requires some investment of our time and effort. But the ratio of the effort expended in relation to the success that is generated makes purchasing foreclosures incredibly worthwhile.

Who Would Be Interested in This Book?

This book is designed especially for the following types of readers nationwide, regardless of experience level, occupation, or financial status:

Renters who wish to purchase a home at an affordable price.

Investors who wish to purchase properties at below-market prices and either fix them up and "flip" them (i.e., sell them) for a quick profit, or keep them and rent them out to tenants while the properties build up equity.

Real estate professionals who wish to help customers and clients buy foreclosures, help defaulting borrowers sell their homes to prevent foreclosure, and/or to help locate sources of bank and government listings to sell to their customers and clients.

Contractors who wish to buy a foreclosure that needs work, complete the repairs at a minimal cost, and then sell it for a profit, or keep it to live in.

Entrepreneurs who wish to build wealth by buying and selling foreclosures for a profit.

Accountants who wish to help their clients buy foreclosures as tax shelters.

Attorneys who want to help their clients purchase foreclosures, or to help their clients who are in danger of defaulting on their home loans to negotiate short sales, or to restructure a defaulting loan to save the client's home from foreclosure.

Parents who wish to learn creative techniques for purchasing real estate with their children.

Landlords who wish to buy foreclosures for use as rental property that yields monthly rental income and yearly income tax deductions.

The list is seemingly endless. . . .

Why This Book Is Unique

I began an extensive career in real estate when I worked for a multifaceted firm that specialized in residential investing, financing, and residential property management. At that time, there was a limited selection of books or courses available to help me get started. Therefore, with no previous experience in the real estate field, I was guided by common sense; an innate ability to react with immediacy and take remedial action when faced with new challenges; trial and error; and the parameters set forth by my industrious, entrepreneurial employers. Thankfully, I didn't make a lot of mistakes—at least, not the same one more than once!

In 1991, with more than a decade of experience under my belt in buying, selling, renting, managing, and creatively financing hundreds of real estate properties, I wanted to make it easier for those who followed in my footsteps. *Buying Real Estate Foreclosures* (first edition) was originally written as a hands-on guidebook that was based on my own real-life experiences. I have been in the trenches, and I have had the same questions, doubts, and feelings of inadequacy that many people encounter when they try something new. I knew that providing easy-to-follow, step-by-step procedures for buying foreclosures could help motivate people who wanted to expand their horizons by instilling in them the confidence they needed to pursue their dreams. From my experience as an investor for myself and my clients, I will help you distinguish a good investment from a poor one. From my experience as real estate broker and a mortgage broker, I will help you find a way to locate the best properties and financing available. From my experience as a professional property manager and as a landlord, I will give you tips for negotiating with people who may presently be occupying, or who may wish to become a tenant in, the foreclosure you purchase. After the first edition of *Buying Real Estate Foreclosures* was published, I attended law school and became a real estate attorney. Drawing from my experience in a daily practice, this third edition includes the latest practical information to help readers understand how to benefit from the most recent state and national foreclosure legislation and identifies the risks and the most common mistakes to avoid in order to protect their interests.

Of course, there are other books on the market for people who wish to buy foreclosures, but this book is unique for three reasons. First, it prepares the reader to buy foreclosures using practical, street-smart techniques. Second, it explains potential legal roadblocks (such as unfriendly occupants and missing legal documents) and gives proven, practical methods for resolving these issues safely and sanely. Third, the book is geared to all levels of experience. Beginners as well as experienced foreclosure purchasers will appreciate the checklists that have been written for every phase of the foreclosure purchase in a logical, organized manner. Beginners will appreciate learning about potential problems they may face before they make costly mistakes, and experienced buyers will relate to the "war stories."

Finding What You Want

The topics in this book have been organized in the following manner:

Understanding foreclosures. The legal procedure behind a fore-closure action is explained to provide readers with an insight into how a lender forecloses on a defaulting borrower. Knowledge of the fore-closure process helps potential buyers identify optimum purchasing opportunities that arise at specific intervals throughout the procedure, recognize certain statutory regulations that may affect purchasing deci-sions, and begin a new venture with a strong foundation to build upon.

Buying foreclosures at the auction. A typical day at an auction is described, including the procedures for buying a foreclosure at an auc-tion; what bidders are expected to do; what bidders may not do; and the step-by-step procedures for bidding on a property, from inspection through closing.

Buying foreclosures after the auction. The opportunities to buy repossessed foreclosures from bank and government agencies are described and defined. This book also uncovers why banks and govern-ment agencies are so highly motivated to sell these properties and the step-by-step negotiating strategies that help you cut through the red tape and rise above your competition. Sources of bank and government agency foreclosure lists (telephone numbers and Web sites) are included to help you get started. Finally, to give readers more of a global perspective, buying foreclosures from a bank's inventory is con-trasted with buying foreclosures at bank auctions.

Buying foreclosures before the auction. The benefits and techniques for finding, approaching, and negotiating with defaulting borrowers before the lender forecloses are revealed and explained.

Financing foreclosures. Readers are taken behind the scenes of a loan application and furnished with loan descriptions and checklists to help them compare the lenders and their loans. Creative strategies are detailed for buyers in four categories: those with limited cash and good credit, those with limited cash and tarnished credit, those with a lot of cash and good credit, and those with a lot of cash and tarnished credit. Partnership strategies and equity sharing options and agreements are also detailed.

Choosing the right property: what you don't know can hurt you. Readers are introduced to the step-by-step procedures, homework, legwork, and research skills that play an essential role in selecting the right property to buy and in calculating the right price to pay.

Preparing your bid sheet. The information that was gathered during the preliminary preparations is organized into one simple bidding form for all kinds of foreclosures to help readers prioritize their wants and needs, finalize their price ranges, and narrow down their selections to those that are most worth pursuing.

Steps to take when your offer is accepted. The five standard operating procedures are explained for buyers when (1) they are the high bidders at auctions; (2) their offer for a bank or government foreclosure is accepted, and (3) they have successfully negotiated the price and terms for preauction foreclosures with defaulting borrowers. Also included is a checklist to help buyers prepare for the closing.

Steps to take after you own the property. Six after-closing tasks and a detailed checklist are provided to help readers complete their foreclosure purchase.

Making repairs to your foreclosure. Two techniques—a "competitive bidding system" and a "payment for performance" initiative—help readers select the right contractor, itemize their specifications, and negotiate the best price and payment terms. It includes sample cost-analysis worksheets, sample bid specifications, and a sample contractor's agreement.

Getting started today. Readers are given six simple steps to turn their dreams into reality today.

Other Major Features in This Book

1. Introductions to each chapter that define its purpose, its context within the overall foreclosure-purchasing process, and how it will help the reader.
2. Thirteen innovative methods for financing foreclosures for each reader's individual situation.
3. Twenty-four questions that will help you distinguish a "dream" foreclosure property from a "disaster."
4. Six hidden additional costs to expect when buying a foreclosure.
5. How to obtain free real estate property values.

6. How to approach angry, unfriendly occupants and get past "the guy with the pit bull and the shotgun."
7. Three lifesaving safety tips.
8. Six steps to take to turn your dreams into reality today.
9. Fifty-two usable sample forms, illustrations, and documents.
10. A bid-calculating worksheet for buying foreclosures safely and sanely, and avoiding "auction fever."
11. Sample form letters that compel a response from reclusive delinquent homeowners and from cooperative and uncooperative occupants living in the foreclosed property that you want to buy.
12. Offer letters to send to banks for REOs in their inventories and techniques for cutting through the red tape when you present your offer.
13. Checklists with procedures for bidding, steps to take after the contract, steps to take after the closing, questions for determining the true value of the property, and steps to take for getting started today.
14. Charts that compare and contrast the differences in purchasing strategies: a traditional purchase versus a bank-auction purchase; a bank-auction purchase versus an REO purchase; purchasing as an investor versus purchasing as an owner-occupant.
15. What the banks can't tell you about the REO properties in their inventories.
16. A Foreclosure Fact Sheet that includes a state-by-state overview of the type of security interest the new owners face in purchasing a foreclosure (mortgage or deed of trust), the time frame in each state for the foreclosing owner to complete the foreclosure action, and the way to locate your state's foreclosure statute to learn even more information about protecting your rights.

Buying
Real Estate
Foreclosures

1
Understanding Foreclosures

Each state in the United States has its own legal procedures for taking foreclosure action. We can, however, find common ground in the basic principles that trigger the commencement of foreclosure actions and in the guidelines that help to control the actions in each state through to their conclusions. In Chapter 1, we introduce the legal procedure that occurs when a lender forecloses, including the definition of a foreclosure action, the types of instruments used to secure loans, the process and duration of judicial and nonjudicial proceedings, and the time frames for foreclosure of defaulting loans in each state. Knowledge of these important issues helps potential buyers (1) identify optimum purchasing opportunities that arise at specific intervals throughout the procedure, (2) recognize certain statutory regulations that may affect purchasing decisions, and (3) begin their new foreclosure venture with a strong foundation to build upon. In upcoming chapters, we bolster this foundation with proven techniques for buying foreclosures safely and sanely.

An Overview of the Legal Procedure in Foreclosure Actions

A foreclosure action is the legal procedure that a lender initiates to reclaim ownership and possession of a property after the borrower fails to repay the loan in accordance with the contractual terms. The foreclosure procedure terminates those rights that the borrower had secured, either through a mortgage or through a deed of trust.

Initially, when a borrower is late with a loan payment, the lender usually attempts to communicate with the borrower (i.e., via a telephone call or letter) to advise the borrower that the loan payment is overdue and to request an explanation for the nonpayment and an opportunity to work out a repayment plan with the borrower. Is the delay temporary? Is the situation that caused the late payment unusual and unlikely to recur? Will the defaulting borrower be able to resume making payments very shortly?

In some states, the mortgage and/or note or the deed of trust also requires the lender to issue a *default notice* advising the borrower that if he or she does not pay the arrears by a certain date, the entire loan balance will be "accelerated." If the lender is not required to send a default notice or to accelerate the loan, the lender may allow the defaulting borrower to reinstate the loan by paying only the late monthly payments. Once the lender accelerates the loan, however, rather than the borrowers owing just the unpaid monthly installments (plus any late charges that have accrued), the entire remaining loan balance becomes due and payable.

As an example (illustrated in Figure 1-1), suppose a borrower obtains a loan with terms that stipulate that the loan will be in default if the borrower is 90 days late in making the monthly loan payment.*

Understanding a Mortgage Loan Default

(*When Loan Terms Allow Foreclosure as a Remedy after Monthly Loan Payments Are 90 Days Late*)

Mortgage Balance—$90,000

Monthly Payment—$ 1,000

❏ The borrower misses 1 payment (30 days late).

At this point the borrower owes $1,000 plus late charges.

❏ The borrower misses the second consecutive payment (60 days late).

At this point the borrower owes $2,000 plus late charges.

❏ The borrower misses the third consecutive payment (90 days late).

At this point the loan balance is accelerated, and the borrower owes the entire remaining balance of $90,000 plus late charges.

Figure 1-1. Understanding a mortgage loan default.

---

* In this book, the terms *defaulting borrower, delinquent homeowner*, and *defaulting homeowner* are used interchangeably because within this context they are synonymous.

In our example, the unpaid loan balance at the time of the default is $90,000 and the borrower's monthly loan payment is $1,000. After missing one monthly payment, the borrower is 30 days late and owes the lender $1,000 (plus late charges). After missing the second consecutive monthly payment, the borrower is 60 days late and owes the lender $2,000 (plus late charges). After missing the third consecutive monthly payment, the borrower is 90 days late. At this point, instead of the borrower's owing the lender $3,000 (plus late charges), the due date of the loan accelerates, in accordance with the 90-day default provision, meaning that the lender may call the entire remaining loan balance of $90,000 due and payable in full. If the borrower in our example is unable to pay the lender the entire loan balance and cannot work out an alternative repayment plan with the lender, the lender may opt to sell the property to the public at an auction in order to recapture its losses. The auction will be held at a designated location that is open to the public, such as the local county courthouse, town hall, or some other such place. The public is notified according to local custom, usually through advertisements published in the town, village, or city newspapers. A court-appointed referee, a sheriff or a trustee is appointed to accept verbal bids on behalf of the foreclosing lender from those who attend the auction and will award the contract of sale to the highest bidder. The initiation of the foreclosure action is guided by the instrument that created the borrower's obligation to repay the loan. All states use either a mortgage or a deed of trust.

Mortgages and Deeds of Trust

Mortgages and deeds of trust are the legal security devices that are executed by the lender and the borrower when the borrower obtains financing from the lender to purchase or refinance real estate. On a nationwide scale, the states are about equally divided in their statutory adoption of mortgages and deeds of trust, and a few states even use both.*

Figure 1-2 is an illustration of a deed of trust, Figure 1-3 is an illustration of a note and mortgage, and Figure 1-4 is a chart illustrating the differences between a mortgage and a deed of trust.

---

* To learn more about the instrument that is used to secure a loan on real property in your state, you can contact your state bar association and ask for the names of attorneys in your area who specialize in real estate and/or foreclosure transactions. Title companies and lending institutions are also sources to contact for more information.

2402
Prepared by the State Bar of Texas for use by lawyers only.
Revised 10/85; 12/87.
© 1987 by the State Bar of Texas

DEED OF TRUST

Date:

Grantor:

Grantor's Mailing Address (including county):

Beneficiary's Rights
　1.　Beneficiary may appoint in writing a substitute or successor trustee, succeeding to all rights and responsibilities of Trustee.
　2.　If the proceeds of the note are used to pay any debt secured by prior liens, Beneficiary is subrogated to all of the rights and liens of the holders of any debt so paid.
　3.　Beneficiary may apply any proceeds received under the insurance policy either to reduce the note or to repair or replace damaged or destroyed improvements covered by the policy.
　4.　If Grantor fails to perform any of Grantor's obligations, Beneficiary may perform those obligations and be reimbursed by Grantor on demand at the place where the note is payable for any sums so paid, including attorney's fees, plus interest on those sums from the dates of payment at the rate stated in the note for matured, unpaid amounts. The sum to be reimbursed shall be secured by this deed of trust.

Trustee's Duties
　If requested by Beneficiary to foreclose this lien, Trustee shall:
　1.　either personally or by agent give notice of the foreclosure sale as required by the Texas Property Code as then amended;
　2.　sell and convey all or part of the property to the highest bidder for cash with a general warranty binding Grantor, subject to prior liens and to other exceptions to conveyance and warranty; and
　3.　from the proceeds of the sale, pay, in this order:
　　　a. expenses of foreclosure, including a commission to Trustee of 5% of the bid;
　　　b. to Beneficiary, the full amount of principal, interest, attorney's fees, and other charges due and unpaid;
　　　c. any amounts required by law to be paid before payment to Grantor; and
　　　d. to Grantor, any balance.

Forms may be obtained through the State Bar of Texas (512) 463-1463

Figure 1-2.　A sample deed of trust.

P 666– Note and Mortgage, short form,
plain English format, 11-78

© 1978 BY JULIUS BLUMBERG, INC.,
PUBLISHER, NYC 10013

CONSULT YOUR LAWYER BEFORE SIGNING THIS FORM–THIS FORM SHOULD BE USED BY LAWYERS ONLY.

NOTE AND MORTGAGE

$................................ Date................................

Parties

Mortgagor

Mortgagee
Address

**Promise
to pay**
principal
amount (debt)
interest
payments

Mortgagor promises to pay to Mortgagee or order the sum of

dollars ($)

with interest at the rate of   % per year from the date above until the debt is paid in full.
Mortgagor will pay the debt as follows:

**Application
of payments**

The Mortgagee will apply each payment first to interest charges and then to repayment of the debt.

**Address
for payment**

Payment shall be made at Mortgagee's address above or at any other address Mortgagee directs.

**Transfer of
rights in
the Property**

Additional promises and agreements of the Mortgagor:

1. The Mortgagor hereby mortgages to the Mortgagee the Property described in this Note and Mortgage. Mortgagor can lose the Property for failure to keep the promises in this Note and Mortgage.

**Property
Mortgaged**

2. The Property mortgaged (the "Property") is All

FORMS MAY BE PURCHASED FROM JULIUS BLUMBERG, Inc.
NY, NY, OR ITS DEALERS. REPRODUCTION PROHIBITED.

Figure 1-3. A sample note and mortgage.

**Comparing Security Instruments Pledged as Collateral
for a Loan on Real Property**

Description	Mortgage	Deed of Trust
The type of security device used to protect the lender's interest	A two-party instrument between the borrower (mortgagor) and the lender (mortgagee)	A three-party instrument between the trustor (borrower), the trustee (an independent third party, generally the title or escrow company), and the beneficiary (lender)
The entity conducting the foreclosure sale	Sheriff or referee (if sale is through the court)	Trustee
The foreclosure procedure	A judge presides over the foreclosure action on the motion of the lender pursuant to preestablished provisions in the mortgage instrument	The trustee makes a finding on the foreclosure action on the motion of the beneficiary pursuant to preestablished provisions in the deed of trust

Figure 1-4. Mortgages vs. deeds of trust.

Understanding Mortgages

In those states in which a mortgage has been adopted as a security instrument (lien theory states), the borrower owns and retains title to real property and the lender holds a mortgage that creates a lien against the borrower's real property. When real property is mortgaged, the borrower signs two separate legal documents, the promissory note (note or bond) and the mortgage. The note is evidence of the borrower's promise to pay the debt and sets forth the monthly loan repayment terms, including the payment amount, the due date, the grace period, the interest rate, default terms, and so on. The mortgage is a two-party instrument executed by the borrower (mortgagor) and the lender (mortgagee) that protects the lender by pledging the real estate that is the subject of the loan as security, or collateral, for the debt. If the borrower fails to make payments as agreed upon under the note, and the borrower is unwilling or unable to bring the payments current, lender has the right to protect its interests by initiating a foreclosure lawsuit to force the sale of the property in order to satisfy the outstanding loan balance.

Understanding Deeds of Trust (Trust Deeds)

In states where deeds of trust (also called *trust deeds*) are adopted as a security instrument (title theory states), these deeds of trust are used in place of mortgages. Deeds of trust are similar to mortgages in that they pledge real property as security for the loan that was taken out by the borrower to purchase the property. However, whereas a mortgage is a two-party instrument between the borrower and the lender, the deed of trust is a three-party instrument between a trustor, a beneficiary, and a trustee. The borrower is called the trustor, and the lender is the beneficiary. The third party, called the trustee, is usually an intermediary with no interest in the property, such as a title or escrow company. The trustee's job is to hold the title to the property in trust for the benefit of, and on behalf of, the beneficiary, as security for the payment of the debt, until such time as the promissory note has been satisfied and the loan paid in full. The trustee reconveys the property to the borrower after the deed of trust is paid in full.

If the loan payment is not brought current, the beneficiary may demand that the trustee initiate foreclosure proceedings to assist the beneficiary in recapturing its losses through money paid by the high bidder at a public auction or through a conveyance of title to the beneficiary if the property is not sold at the auction.

Judicial and Nonjudicial Foreclosures

While mortgages and deeds of trust are the security devices that establish the borrowers' obligations to repay their loans, if a borrower defaults on these obligations, there are two types of legal actions that may be commenced by the lender to cause the property to be sold at a public sale and, hopefully, to bring enough proceeds to pay the unpaid loan balance in full. Such actions, set forth by each state's foreclosure statute, are known as *judicial* or *nonjudicial* foreclosures.

A state's adoption of a judicial or a nonjudicial foreclosure statute affects two important issues: (1) the duration of the foreclosure proceeding and (2) the legal process that must be followed from commencement to completion of that proceeding. The differences can be significant. For example, the amount of time it takes a lender to foreclose on a delinquent loan in a state that has adopted the judicial approach to foreclosures is much longer than the amount of time it takes a lender to foreclose in a state that has adopted a nonjudicial approach. A judicial foreclosure is more cumbersome and takes longer to complete because it requires the foreclosing lender to initiate a lawsuit through the court system to obtain a judgment of foreclosure and sale. By contrast, a nonjudicial foreclosure, through its *power of sale clause*, can be completed in a fraction of the time it takes for a judicial foreclosure because, if a borrower defaults on repaying a loan, no lengthy court action is required by the lender—the property is advertised and sold quickly in accordance with the procedure prescribed by each state's foreclosure statute.

Some states have adopted a judical statute for all foreclosure proceedings; others have adopted a nonjudicial statute. Still other states have adopted a combination of the two statutes and allow judicial foreclosure proceedings for residential properties and nonjudicial proceedings for commercial properties. The length of time it takes for a lender to foreclose can have a dramatic impact on a buyer's foreclosure purchasing strategy. For example, in a nonjudicial foreclosure state, a buyer who wishes to purchase a preforeclosure before the auction would implement a more expeditious plan of action because of the abbreviated time frame available to complete the transaction. On the other hand, a buyer who wishes to purchase a preforeclosure in a judicial foreclosure state generally has more time, and therefore can implement a more leisurely plan of action.

In the next paragraphs, we look at the procedural differences in judicial and nonjudicial foreclosures.

The Judicial Foreclosure Procedure

In states in which a judicial foreclosure procedure is utilized, if the borrower is unable (or unwilling) to bring the loan payments current, the lender forwards the file to its attorney and authorizes the attorney to initiate a lawsuit to enforce the lender's rights pursuant to the mortgage or the deed of trust. The judicial process (derived from the word *judge*) is held in a courtroom venue and presided over by a court judge. The foreclosing lender's attorney orders a *foreclosure search*, which is similar to a report from a title company; it provides the attorney with information about the property owner and the mortgage or deed of trust instrument pledged as the security interest. In addition, the lender ascertains that the party named as the defendant in the foreclosure proceeding is, in fact, the current legal property owner of record.

Other creditors with an interest in the property are located and named as defendants in the action, including the trustee holding the deed of trust, second mortgagees, mechanic's lien holders, judgment holders, utility companies, and federal and state income tax and property tax lien holders.

Next, the attorney prepares the legal documents for the lawsuit, including a *summons* (the notice directing the defendant to appear in court), a *complaint* (the plaintiff's allegations of entitlement to relief and the relief sought), and a *lis pendens* (also known as a notice of pendancy), which is the legal document that "gives notice to the world that there is a legal action pending on this property which may affect the title."

The required documents are filed with the clerk of the court in the county in which the property is located, and an *index number* is purchased to bring the action to the court's calendar. The index number will be used to identify the action and will appear on all future notices, advertisements, and legal filings relating to this case. In many jurisdictions, anyone who wishes to view the legal file, which contains the paperwork associated with this action, would requisition the file by the index number. Once the lis pendens is filed, the public is on notice that there is an action pending on this property. Any future liens or judgments filed against the property after the lis pendens was filed may be excluded from the foreclosure action, and those creditors will have to initiate legal proceedings against the delinquent owner's assets independently.

After the lender's attorney files the necessary documents with the court, all parties named as defendants in the action (including the delinquent borrower, the creditors, tenants of the owner, trustees, and anyone else involved) must be served with the legal documents so that their interests may be terminated by the foreclosure action. Each state has enacted statutes that regulate the time frames within which legal documents must be served on the defendants and proof of service filed with the courts. Some states also require tenants living in the premises (if any) to be named as parties to the action and served with notice in order to terminate an existing lease. If the tenants are not named, the new owner may be required to honor the terms of the preexisting lease.

If the borrower fails to respond to the complaint within the statutory time limit, the attorney submits a report to the court stating the facts of the case and requesting the court to appoint a referee or sheriff. The referee/sheriff reviews the facts and circumstances in the foreclosure action and renders his or her report to the court. The judge then issues a Judgment of Foreclosure and Sale in favor of the foreclosing lender.

The auction sale is advertised in accordance with local statutes. At the auction, the referee/sheriff reads the *Terms of Sale* to the public and starts the bidding at the "upset price," also known as the "opening bid amount" or the "the dollar bid," which is the amount set forth by the courts in the Judgment of Foreclosure and Sale plus any amounts required to be included by the state's foreclosure statute that have accrued between the Judgment of Foreclosure date and the auction date (for example, interest and unpaid property taxes, foreclosure costs, legal fees, and so on).

The step-by-step procedures for a judicial foreclosure action are illustrated in Figure 1-5.

A JUDICIAL FORECLOSURE ACTION

Step 1.   The borrower defaults on repaying the loan.

Step 2.   If required, the lender issues a default notice and accelerates the loan.

Step 3.   The lender's attorney begins the foreclosure lawsuit.

Step 4.   The lender's attorney prepares the necessary foreclosure documents pursuant to statutory requirements.

Step 5.   The lender's attorney serves the summons and complaint/lis pendens on the defaulting borrower and additional parties named as defendants.

Step 6.   The lender's attorney purchases an index number, which will be used to identify this action in future proceedings.

Step 7.   The court judge appoints a referee or sheriff to review the facts and circumstances and render a report.

Step 8.   The court issues the Judgment of Foreclosure and Sale and the Order of Publication.

Step 9.   The lender's attorney advertises the upcoming auction in accordance with local custom.

Step 10.   The property is offered for sale at a public auction.

Step 11.   Either the property is purchased at the auction by a new owner or title is conveyed back to the foreclosing lender if no one buys it at the auction.

Step 12.   The borrowers may exercise any statutory rights of redemption after the auction.

Step 13.   The referee or sheriff's deed is given to the high bidder or foreclosing lender after the statutory redemption period expires.

Figure 1-5.   Steps in a judicial foreclosure action.

The Nonjudicial Foreclosure Procedure

In states where a nonjudicial foreclosure procedure is used to foreclose a mortgage or a deed of trust, instead of commencing a lawsuit to foreclose on the defaulting borrower, the foreclosing mortgage lender or deed of trust beneficiary invokes the *power of sale* clause pursuant to a covenant in the mortgage or deed of trust.

If the borrower does not repay the loan in accordance with the terms of the mortgage or deed of trust, the power of sale clause allows a lender holding a mortgage or a trustee holding a deed of trust to sell the property at a public auction without a court or judge's involvement. The nonjudicial procedure is less costly and time consuming than its judicial counterpart because it occurs under the supervision of a trustee and does not require a lawsuit. The lender or trustee simply records a notice of default and sends a copy to the borrower or to the trustor; after the statutory period, a notice of sale is posted on the property.

The step-by-step procedures for a nonjudicial foreclosure action are illustrated in Figure 1-6.

A NONJUDICIAL FORECLOSURE ACTION

Step 1. The borrower defaults on repaying the loan.

Step 2. The beneficiary instructs the trustee named in the deed of trust to file a notice of default with the appropriate county or public official's office in the county where the premises are located.

Step 3. The public trustee advertises the upcoming sale in accordance with local custom.

Step 4. Either the property is purchased at the auction by a new owner or title is conveyed back to the foreclosing lender if the property is not sold at the auction.

Step 5. The borrowers may exercise any statutory rights of redemption after the auction.

Step 6. The trustee's deed is given to the high bidder or foreclosing lender after the statutory redemption period expires.

Figure 1-6. Steps in a nonjudicial foreclosure action.

Finding the Foreclosure Statute in Your State

Each state has its own foreclosure statute governing such issues as its legal procedure, required legal notices, necessary versus permissible defendants, the defaulting borrowers' right of redemption, deficiency judgments, payment of surplus funds, filing requirements, and other such factors. The foreclosure laws for each state are only a click away on the Internet. Using a search engine such as yahoo.com, google.com, msn.com, or aol.com, simply type in the name of your state and the words "foreclosure statute" or "foreclosure laws."

A chart with a compilation of foreclosure details for each state, including the security interests (mortgage or deed of trust), foreclosure type (judicial or nonjudicial), foreclosure time frame (months for completing a foreclosure action), and foreclosure statutes adopted by each state, is given in Figure 1-7.

State	Security Interest	Foreclosure Type	Foreclosure Time Frame (in months)	Foreclosure Statute
Alabama	Mortgage	Nonjudicial	3	§ 35-10-1
Alaska	Deed of trust	Nonjudicial	4	§ 34.20.090
Arizona	Deed of trust	Nonjudicial	3	§ 33.807
Arkansas	Mortgage	Judicial	3	§ 51-1106
California	Deed of trust	Nonjudicial	4	§ 2924
Colorado	Deed of trust	Nonjudicial	5	§ 38-37-113
Connecticut	Mortgage	Nonjudicial	6	§ 49-24
Delaware	Mortgage	Judicial	7	§ 2101
District of Columbia	Deed of trust	Nonjudicial	4	§ 45-701
Florida	Mortgage	Judicial	7	§ 702.01
Georgia	Mortgage	Nonjudicial	3	§ 44-14-162
Hawaii	Mortgage	Nonjudicial	7	§ 667-1
Idaho	Deed of trust	Nonjudicial	9	§ 45-1506
Illinois	Mortgage	Judicial	10	§ 15-1101
Indiana	Mortgage	Judicial	9	§ 32-29-7
Iowa	Mortgage	Judicial	7	§ 654.1
Kansas	Mortgage	Judicial	4	§ 60-2410

(cont.)

Figure 1-7. State-by-state foreclosure facts.

Kentucky	Mortgage	Judicial	7	§ 426.190
Louisiana	Mortgage	Judicial	6	§ 2293
Maine	Mortgage	Judicial	10	§ 14-6321
Maryland	Deed of trust	Nonjudicial	5	§ 7-101
Massachusetts	Mortgage	Judicial	5	§ 244.1
Michigan	Mortgage	Nonjudicial	3	§ 451.401
Minnesota	Mortgage	Nonjudicial	4	§ 580.01
Mississippi	Deed of trust	Nonjudicial	4	§ 89-1-55
Missouri	Deed of trust	Nonjudicial	3	§ 443.325
Montana	Deed of trust	Nonjudicial	6	§ 71-1-221
Nebraska	Mortgage	Judicial	4	§ 76-1005
Nevada	Deed of trust	Nonjudicial	4	§ 40.425
New Hampshire	Mortgage	Nonjudicial	3	§ 479.19
New Jersey	Mortgage	Judicial	10	§ 2A-50-2
New Mexico	Mortgage	Judicial	5	§ 48-7-7
New York	Mortgage	Judicial	10	§ 1301-91
North Carolina	Deed of trust	Judicial	2	§ 45
North Dakota	Mortgage	Judicial	4	§ 32-19-01
Ohio	Mortgage	Judicial	8	§ 2323.07
Oklahoma	Mortgage	Judicial	7	§ 46.42
Oregon	Deed of trust	Nonjudicial	5	§ 88
Pennsylvania	Mortgage	Judicial	9	§ 91.135
Rhode Island	Mortgage	Nonjudicial	3	§ 34-11-22
South Carolina	Mortgage	Judicial	6	§15-7-10
South Dakota	Mortgage	Judicial	4	§ 21-47-1
Tennessee	Deed of trust	Nonjudicial	3	§ 35-501
Texas	Deed of trust	Nonjudicial	2	§ 51.002
Utah	Deed of trust	Nonjudicial	5	§ 78.37-1
Vermont	Mortgage	Judicial	10	§ 4526
Virginia	Deed of trust	Nonjudicial	4	§ 55-59.1
Washington	Deed of trust	Nonjudicial	5	§ 61.12.010
West Virginia	Deed of trust	Nonjudicial	4	§ 38-1-3
Wisconsin	Mortgage	Judicial	10	§ 846.01
Wyoming	Mortgage	Judicial	3	§ 34-4-101

Figure 1-7. State-by-state foreclosure facts (*continued*).

The Soldier's and Sailor's Civil Relief Act of 1940

In some cases, a lender must modify a foreclosure action in order to comply with the Soldier's and Sailor's Civil Relief Act of 1940 (the Act). Under the Act, when property is owned by a person who is on active military duty and the loan was originated prior to the commencement of that military duty, then no sale, foreclosure, or seizure of property for nonpayment of any sum due will be valid if it is made during the period of the military service or within several months thereafter. This does not apply if the courts find that the ability of the defaulting borrower to comply with the terms of the loan obligation is not materially affected by the borrower's involvement in military service or if the foreclosure sale was granted by the courts before the active duty began. Under the Act, active-duty military personnel may be allowed a reduction of interest rates on debts, including mortgages and deeds of trust, if their involvement in military service impairs their ability to pay their loans at the current interest rates. Repayment plans and extensions of time to pay can also be negotiated. Be aware that when a defaulting serviceman or servicewoman is protected under the Act, foreclosure sales may be delayed and/or bidders prevented from completing their transactions.

The Three Opportunities for Purchasing Foreclosures

Now that we know how a property finds its way to the foreclosure auction, in the chapters that follow, we will uncover the opportunities, understand the benefits, and avoid the risks associated with buying real estate foreclosures in today's marketplace.

1. At the Auction (Chapter 2)

The borrower has defaulted on the loan payments, and the lender is seeking to recapture its losses by offering the property for sale at a public auction.

2. After the Auction (Chapters 3 and 4)

Lending institutions and government agencies sell repossessed foreclosures in their inventories to the public.

3. Before the Auction (Chapter 5)

Defaulting borrowers who are about to be foreclosed on try to avoid losing their equity, their credit rating, and even their future income by selling the property before the lender forecloses on it.

2

The Basics of Buying Foreclosures at the Auction

The first opportunity for purchasing foreclosures that we will cover is found at foreclosure auctions. Foreclosure auctions are court-ordered sales through which the maker of a loan that is in default seeks to recapture its losses by selling the property to the highest bidder. In Chapter 2, we describe what to expect on a typical day at a foreclosure auction. Understanding the overall procedure will help buyers determine if foreclosure auctions are the best opportunity available for reaching their personal financial goals.

A Day at the Auction

To put this event into perspective, we are at a point in the foreclosure process where the borrower has defaulted on a loan secured by a mortgage or a deed of trust and the lender is seeking to recapture its losses by offering the property for sale to the public at an auction.

An Overview of Auctions

There are three kinds of auctions that sellers in general use to convey real and/or personal property. An *absolute auction* is a type of auction in which the seller must accept the highest bid, no matter how low it is. This type of auction poses a risk to the seller, especially when the high bid is lower than the market value of the item and is more suitable for events such as an auction of personal property at a charitable event.

The next type of auction, an *auction with reservation* is one in which, in contrast to an absolute auction, the seller reserves the right to reject any offer from a bidder, no matter how lucrative that offer may be.

Finally, a *minimum bid auction* is one in which the seller establishes a starting amount to begin the bidding. All bids must exceed that amount, and the highest bidder is awarded the contract. This is the type of auction that is conducted for foreclosure sales.

To begin a typical day at a foreclosure auction, let's review the overall minimum bid auction procedure.

The Opening Bid Amount

Before the foreclosure auction commences, the opening bid amount, also known as the upset price, dollar bid, or credit bid, has been established to begin the bidding. The opening bid amount usually includes the unpaid mortgage balance, interest and back taxes, court costs, and legal fees. These debts are normally satisfied at the closing with the money paid by the successful high bidder.

The Bidding Procedure

When I attended my first foreclosure sale, I had visions of an auctioneer wielding a huge gavel and yodeling bid amounts from behind an oversized podium. Instead, I was surprised to find that, after the auctioneer announced that the foreclosure sale was about to begin, verbal bidding was conducted in a quiet and organized manner—with no yodeling and no gavel!

Although many people attend auctions, not everyone is there to bid on a property. Some people go to auctions merely out of curiosity. Others go to familiarize themselves with the auction procedure before they bid, to reduce the intimidation factor that arises when people are about to embark on a new venture.

At some foreclosure auctions, you may find yourself in a bidding war with 10 other people; in such a case, the person making the highest offer will be awarded the contract for the purchase of the property. On the other hand, you may find that you are the only person attending the auction. Should this happen, you will be able to buy the property at the opening bid amount because there are no competitors there to bid up the price.

When the auction begins, the auctioneer (court-appointed referee, sheriff, or trustee) explains the bidding procedure to be followed and describes the property (or properties) up for bid. By "describe," I mean that the auctioneer recites the legal description of the property and any related tax map designations. Details such as distinctive structural features that make the property more attractive to a buyer (e.g., professional landscaping, outdoor hot tub, in-ground pool, or central air-conditioning) are not mentioned because they are not considered relevant to the legal description. Later, in Chapter 9, we will look at how to inspect a foreclosure before you purchase it. Ideally, the improvements to the property should be identified and evaluated as part of your prebid preparations.

Statutory provisions govern the procedures that are used at foreclosure auctions. In some states, auctions are conducted through oral bidding, in which the bidder orally offers the amount that he or she wishes to pay for the foreclosed property. Another method used for bidding at auctions involves sealed written offers. The written offers are given to the designated authority, who opens them and announces the successful high bidder's name and bid amount. Some auction regulations require bidders to register before the auction, at which time they must provide proof that, if they are the high bidders, they have with them the financial resources necessary (usually 10 percent of the high bid) to make the down payment. Attending the mortgage or trust deed auctions in your locality to familiarize yourself with the bidding process is an essential prerequisite for preparing to buy foreclosures at auctions and is discussed in more detail in Chapter 14.

The High Bidder

The high bidder is usually awarded the equivalent of a contract of sale. If you, as the high bidder, are awarded the contract, you will be expected to render a required down payment (usually 10 percent of the bid amount) immediately in the form of a money order, bank check, or certified funds, as required by the court-appointed referee, sheriff, or trustee. (In Chapter 9, we review the people to contact to obtain the down payment information, and in Chapter 10, as part of your prebid preparations, we cover how to calculate the 10 percent down payment to bring with you.)

Thirty Days to Close in Bank Auctions

You will be expected to "close" with the 90 percent balance due within a certain period of time—usually 30 days after the contract is signed at the auction. Under certain circumstances, you may be granted an extension (extra time to close). For example, if your attorney is on vacation, you may need to ask for an extension until he or she returns. Normally, however, if you are the successful high bidder at a foreclosure auction, you will be expected to close within the 30-day period stipulated in the contract.

Unusual Closing Delays

I was once involved in an unusual situation in which the referee appointed by the court to sell the property at the auction required an extension of more than a year because a necessary legal document was missing. Before I explain the details of this case at greater length, some background information on the nature of the document in question is in order.

In many states, real property is conveyed through either a deed (see Figure 2-1) or a *Torrens title* (see Figure 2-2), also known as an "Owner's

CONSULT YOUR LAWYER BEFORE SIGNING THIS INSTRUMENT—THIS INSTRUMENT SHOULD BE USED BY LAWYERS ONLY.

THIS INDENTURE, made the   day of   , nineteen hundred and

BETWEEN

party of the first part, and

party of the second part,

WITNESSETH, that the party of the first part, in consideration of Ten Dollars and other valuable consideration paid by the party of the second part, does hereby grant and release unto the party of the second part, the heirs or successors and assigns of the party of the second part forever,

ALL that certain plot, piece or parcel of land, with the buildings and improvements thereon erected, situate, lying and being in the

TOGETHER with all right, title and interest, if any, of the party of the first part in and to any streets and roads abutting the above described premises to the center lines thereof; TOGETHER with the appurtenances and all the estate and rights of the party of the first part in and to said premises; TO HAVE AND TO HOLD the premises herein granted unto the party of the second part, the heirs or successors and assigns of the party of the second part forever.

AND the party of the first part covenants that the party of the first part has not done or suffered anything whereby the said premises have been encumbered in any way whatever, except as aforesaid.

AND the party of the first part, in compliance with Section 13 of the Lien Law, covenants that the party of the first part will receive the consideration for this conveyance and will hold the right to receive such consideration as a trust fund to be applied first for the purpose of paying the cost of the improvement and will apply the same first to the payment of the cost of the improvement before using any part of the total of the same for any other purpose. The word "party" shall be construed as if it read "parties" whenever the sense of this indenture so requires.

IN WITNESS WHEREOF, the party of the first part has duly executed this deed the day and year first above written.

IN PRESENCE OF:

FORMS MAY BE PURCHASED FROM JULIUS BLUMBERG, INC., NY, NY OR ANY OF ITS DEALERS. REPRODUCTION PROHIBITED.

Standard N.Y.B.T.U. Form 8002. Bargain and Sale Deed, with Covenant Against Grantor's Acts—Individual or Corporation.

Figure 2-1. A standard deed.

THE LAND TITLE REGISTRATION LAW

Owner's Duplicate Certificate of Title

No. 99632	FIRST REGISTERED April 23. 1949
TRANSFER FROM	CERTIFICATE No. 92073

I, LESTER M. ALBERTSON, Registrar of the County of Suffolk, in the State of New York, DO HEREBY CERTIFY THAT

of

are the owners of an Estate
in the following Land: ALL that certain plot, piece or parcel of land, with the buildings and improvement thereon erected, situate, lying and being in the Town of Islip, County of Suffolk, State of New York, known and designated at a certain map entitled, "Map of Islip Park Estates developed by Frederick Farms Inc., 258 Broadway, N.Y.C., surveyed by George H. Walbridge C.E. and Surveyor, Babylon, N.Y." and filed in the Suffolk County Clerk's Office on Map No. 1717 on November 25, 1949 as all by Lot No. 96 being bounded and described as follows BEGINNING at a point on the easterly side of Bay Shore Avenue at a point distant 200.00 feet northerly as measured along the easterly side of Bay Shore Avenue from the corner formed by the intersection of its intersection with the northerly side of Belmont Street; running thence north 0 degree 02 minutes 10 seconds west along the easterly side of Bay Shore Avenue 60 feet; thence north 89 degrees 57 minutes 50 seconds east 178.00 feet; thence south 0 degrees 02 minutes 10 seconds east 60 feet; thence south 89 degrees 57 minutes 50 seconds west 178.00 feet to the easterly side of Bay Shore Avenue at the point or place of BEGINNING.

SUBJECT to the estates, easements, encumbrances and charges hereunder noted.

WITNESS my hand and official seal at
Riverhead, N.Y., this 19th day November, 1975.

Lester M. Albertson
Registrar

Figure 2-2. A Torrens title.

Duplicate Certificate of Title" (ODC). Torrens titles originated many years ago in Australia as the method used in that country to record real property transactions. However, deeds and Torrens titles are not always interchangeable documents.

An original Torrens title is manila-colored and has a gold seal on the front page. Also on the front page is a legal description of the property, just as in a deed. But, unlike a deed, the Torrens title contains a listing of the *memorials* that includes all the legal instruments (mortgages, liens, judgments, and satisfactions) that have been recorded on the property from its origins.

The deed or Torrens title, depending on which of the two is used, will be among the important documents sent to a new homeowner after it is recorded. From that point on, if a homeowner loses a deed, it can be replaced for a few dollars simply by requesting a duplicate copy from the office of the county clerk in the county where the property is located. If a homeowner loses a Torrens title, however, in many states a court order may be required to replace it with another original Torrens title. This procedure can take many months, and, as I mentioned, in one foreclosure purchase in which I was involved, it took well over a year! In states where the Torrens system has not been simplified, when property under a Torrens title is conveyed, the original document must be updated to reflect the details of the new transaction [i.e., the seller's mortgage loan satisfaction, the purchaser's name(s), new mortgagee information, and other such data]. Because the original Torrens title is most likely in the possession of the defaulting borrower who is about to be foreclosed on, it is often difficult for the foreclosing lender to obtain the document. Predictably, the defaulting borrower is unwilling to cooperate with the foreclosing lender by making the document available because this would expedite the sale of the borrower's home to someone else. If the original document cannot be obtained, the foreclosing lender may have to go through the courts to get a replacement Torrens title in order to convey the property to the successful high bidder.

That having been said, we can return now to the case with the missing documents. In that situation, the delay occurred because the foreclosing lender was unable to obtain the original Torrens title from the defaulting borrower. As a result, the successful high bidder (an investor for whom I was managing the property) had to wait more than a year until the referee was able to obtain a replacement for the original Torrens title through the courts. The investor ended up benefiting from the experience because he had plenty of time to secure financing and work out a rental agreement with the occupants. This is not to imply that the procedure for obtaining a new Torrens title will always take as long as it did in this case. Your state may have legislation that makes it unnecessary for a lender without the original Torrens certificate to go through the courts for a new one. Contact your attorney or a title expert for more information on whether the Torrens system is operative in the areas in which you wish to purchase foreclosures.

Warning: Peculiar Purchase Ahead

Foreclosure auction purchases are different from a traditional purchase involving a buyer and a seller. In some states, if the foreclosure statutes and customary procedures allow, you can ask the referee, sheriff, or trustee to provide you with the Terms of Sale, which set forth the procedures and define the legalities for purchasing foreclosures at a particular auction. Whether or not this document exists, you should prepare yourself in advance to ascertain whether the foreclosure you wish to purchase is the best choice for you. Let's look at the distinguishing characteristics that make foreclosure auction purchases unique.

Buying for Less than Market Value

Normally, you pay close to market value, or maybe a little less, for a traditional property purchase. For a foreclosure purchased at an auction, however, you could end up paying a small fraction of the price you would have paid for a traditional purchase, because the purchase price is based on the unpaid loan balance and not on the market value.

I know of an investor who purchased a property at an auction in Westhampton Beach on Long Island, New York, that was worth approximately $1 million ... for $167,000! He was the only bidder at the auction, and he bought the foreclosure for one dollar over the upset price. The auction just happened to take place on the day of a hurricane! While this is certainly an extreme example, many seasoned foreclosure purchasers vow that the best time to bid on a property is during poor weather conditions, when fewer people venture outside to attend an auction!

No Down Payment Refunds

In a traditional purchase, there is usually a contingency clause, also known as a mortgage contingency clause, included in the sales contract whereby, if you are unable to obtain financing from a lender to purchase the property, you are entitled to have your down payment refunded. However, when a foreclosure is purchased at an auction, there is no contingency clause allowing down payment refunds. If you cannot come up with the cash required to complete the transaction within the contractual 30-day period, you could lose your down payment.

Check with the referee, sheriff, or trustee and/or have your attorney examine the Terms of Sale to confirm that the down payment itself would be considered the total amount of "liquidated damages" and that you would not be held responsible for the difference between your original bid amount and the reauctioned amount if the property was subsequently sold for less money.

A man who attended one of my seminars on buying foreclosures told me that he was planning to participate in his first auction the following day. He intended to bring his family's life savings with him to use as his down payment if he was the successful high bidder. He didn't realize that the contract would require him to close with the 90 percent balance due within 30 days; he expected the referee to wait for him to obtain financing in order to close—even if it took several months. He literally turned pale and broke out into a cold sweat when he learned how close he had come to losing everything.

The Burden of Dispossessing Occupants

In a traditional purchase, you can expect the premises to be "broom clean" and vacant on the closing date, unless other arrangements have been made in advance between the buyer and the seller (for example, a postclosing possession agreement allowing the seller to remain there for a couple of days after the new owner takes title at the closing). When you buy a foreclosure at an auction, however, the burden of dispossessing any of the current occupants falls on the high bidder, after the closing has taken place.

Buying in "As-Is" Condition

Another distinction between purchases of properties at foreclosure auctions and traditional purchases involves representations about the property's condition. In a traditional purchase, you expect the plumbing, heating, electrical systems, and appliances to be in good working order, and the roof to be free of leaks. Because foreclosure proceedings are indicative of a distressed situation, you cannot expect the same representations that the property is in good repair. Foreclosure purchases are sold in "as-is" condition. What you see, or don't see, is what you get—or don't get! People who are losing their homes are not likely to keep up with repairs or cosmetic appearances. You must remember that when you are buying a foreclosure, you are not dealing with a traditional seller whose contract terms usually require the property to be sold in good condition. Instead, you are dealing with an entity, the lending institution, and the referee's, sheriff's, or trustee's sole function is to sell the property at the highest price possible in order to mitigate the lender's losses.

The Defaulting Borrower's Right of Redemption

Another foreclosure auction idiosyncrasy is the defaulting borrower's right of redemption. The right of redemption is available to everyone who owns real estate; in the foreclosure auction context, it allows the defaulting borrower to reclaim his property by paying the entire outstanding debt (the upset price) up until the moment that the public auction begins.

In some states, the defaulting borrower's right of redemption allows him to reclaim his property from the high bidder even after the auction by paying the upset price plus interest. In other states, the defaulting borrower's right of redemption expires once the bidding begins, in which case the only way the borrower can reclaim the property is by being the successful high bidder. Depending on the state you live in, there may or may not be a right of redemption period. If there is such a period, it can vary from a few months up to a year. The Internal Revenue Service has 120 days after a foreclosure auction sale to redeem property to which a federal tax lien has been attached. If your state has a redemption period, the new owner cannot sell the property until the redemption period expires. Check with your attorney or title expert to confirm the redemption procedures that apply in your state.

Unanticipated Liens You May Be Responsible for in Addition to the Purchase Price

In a traditional purchase, you can expect the property you are purchasing to have no outstanding liens, except for the financing you borrowed to purchase it. On the other hand, when you purchase a foreclosure at an auction, there may be unexpected liens that you are responsible for, in addition to the purchase price.

For example, if the foreclosure action is on a senior lien (i.e., a first mortgage), no problem; the high bidder takes the premises free and clear of junior liens. The lienholders in second (and third or lower) position would have to recover the outstanding amounts due from the defaulting borrower personally, by filing an independent action for a judgment against him and seizing other assets he may own in the county. (This is why junior liens are so much more expensive than senior liens—borrowers are really paying for the greater risk of loss that second lienholders incur.)

By contrast, if the foreclosure action is on a junior lien, the high bidder takes the premises *subject to* the senior lien, meaning that, in this case, the senior lien balance is another expense that must be taken into consideration as part of the purchase price. Prospective bidders who have done their homework are aware that they are bidding on a junior lien. Some people work out an assumption of the senior lien balance with the senior lienholder; other people simply apply for enough new financing to cover the amount needed to pay off both the senior and junior liens.

To illustrate these concepts, let's compare how you would be affected if you were bidding at an auction on a property where the senior lienholder was foreclosing, and another where the junior lienholder was foreclosing. In both situations, let's assume that the market value of the property is $250,000. Also assume that the remaining balance on the senior lien is $100,000 and the remaining balance on the junior lien is $50,000. Now, let's look at what happened when the property owner experienced financial difficulty and could afford to pay only one, but not both, of the two loans.

If the borrower paid only the junior lienholder, the senior lienholder would foreclose. The upset price to begin the auction would be $100,000 (the unpaid balance of the senior lien) plus legal fees and other such costs. To simplify our illustration, let's say that you are the only bidder at the auction (so no one bids up the price), and that you are awarded the contract for $100,000 (plus legal fees and other such costs). You take the property free and clear of the junior lien. (As stated earlier, the junior lienholder must recapture its losses by filing liens against other assets owned by the defaulting borrower.) As the successful high bidder for this foreclosure, you purchased a property valued at $250,000 for $100,000.

On the other hand, if the borrower paid only the senior lien and could not afford to pay the junior lien, it is the junior lienholder that is foreclosing. The upset price is $50,000 (the unpaid balance of the junior lien) plus legal fees and other such costs. Again, let's say that you are the only bidder at the auction, and that you are awarded the contract for $50,000 (plus legal fees and other costs). You are the new owner of the premises, subject to the senior lien (of $100,000). Either you negotiate with the senior lienholder to assume the balance of the loan in your name and make monthly payments over an agreed-upon period of years, or, if the senior lienholder requires payment in full, you will have to apply for enough financing to cover your $50,000 high bid on the junior lien, plus $100,000 to pay off the existing senior lien. As the successful high bidder for this junior lien foreclosure, you purchased a property valued at $250,000 for $150,000.

In cases where the high bid amount at the auction exceeds the upset price, the overage (a.k.a. "surplus") goes to pay off the junior lienholders and other creditors. If there are no other lienholders, the surplus goes to the defaulting borrower.

There are several ways for foreclosure purchasers to determine whether the foreclosure action is on a senior or a junior lien, depending on your experience level. The most foolproof method (and the one that I recommend for foreclosure purchasers who are not experienced title professionals) is to hire a title company to perform a "last owner search," also known as a "lien and judgment search." Much less extensive (and much less costly) than a title search, the "last owner" search provides an accurate summary of the instruments that affect the property, and it is the best way to ensure that you have the correct information about the position (first, second, third, etc.) of the lien that you are bidding on. Going forward, if you are the high bidder, you will most likely want to order a full title report, but until you know that you are the high bidder, why take on the expense of a full title report?

Contact your attorney or a title company for more information about this type of search.

If you know your way around the county clerk's office and are familiar with real property documents, you can search the public records to see whether more than one lien has been recorded on the property that you are interested in. If there is more than one lien, the first one recorded is usually the first secured lien, except in cases where a subordination agreement was filed.

You can requisition the foreclosure file from the government office in the county where the action arose. Look for wording in the legal documents indicating that the foreclosure is on a "purchase money" loan. If so, the mortgage or deed of trust was given as security for the loan when the defaulting borrower originally purchased the property (as opposed to a refinancing or a second mortgage loan), and you will most likely be bidding on a first mortgage.

Figure 2-3 compares and contrasts the characteristics that distinguish foreclosure auction purchases from traditional purchases.

Finding Upcoming Foreclosure Auctions

Foreclosure Auction List Publications

There are companies that publish lists of upcoming foreclosure auctions in the form of newspapers, magazines, or newsletters. These lists

BUYING A PROPERTY FROM A TRADITIONAL SELLER VERSUS BUYING A FORECLOSURE AT A BANK AUCTION

BUYING A PROPERTY FROM A TRADITIONAL SELLER	BUYING A FORECLOSURE AT A BANK AUCTION
1. The asking price is based on market value.	1. The asking price is based on the unpaid loan balance plus expenses.
2. The contract terms normally include a "financing contingency clause" (a.k.a. "mortgage contingency clause").	2. The contract terms do not include a "financing contingency clause" (a.k.a. "mortgage contingency clause").
3. The premises are conveyed in "broom clean" and vacant condition.	3. The burden of evicting the current occupants is on the new owner, after the property is conveyed.
4. The plumbing, heating, and electrical systems and the appliances are in working order, and the roof is free of leaks.	4. The plumbing, heating, and electrical systems and the appliances and roof are sold in "as-is" condition.
5. The seller has no right of redemption after the property is conveyed to the new owner.	5. The defaulting borrower's right of redemption may extend beyond the auction date.
6. The seller usually clears up any existing title problems (i.e., liens and judgments on the premises) before the property is conveyed to the new owner.	6. The new owner may be responsible for additional liens and judgments in addition to the purchase price.
7. The manner of making an offer to purchase the property is by oral or written offer to the seller or the seller's agent.	7. The manner of making an offer to purchase the property is by oral bidding at a public foreclosure auction.

Figure 2-3. Buying a property from a traditional seller vs. buying a property at a bank foreclosure auction.

are also available to subscribers who wish to purchase them through the Internet.

Answers to the following questions can help you decide which fore-closure list provider offers the best services for the best price.

What information is included in the publication? Obviously, the more information supplied to you, the subscriber, the better. Here are some of the features I have found to be most helpful:

- A picture of the property
- The number of rooms in the property
- The dimensions of the rooms
- The appraised value
- The lot size
- Whether the foreclosure action is on a junior or senior lien
- Whether or not the property is registered by deed or by Torrens title (if applicable)
- The property address
- Directions to the auction location
- Time, place, and date of the auction
- The current mortgage balance
- The name of the foreclosing lender
- The lender's attorney information (name, address, and telephone number)
- The referee, sheriff, or trustee information (name, address, and telephone number)
- The index number of the action

What states/counties/towns does the publication cover? If you are inter-ested in properties that are located in more than one county or town-ship, you need to know whether they are all included in the publication. On the other hand, if you are interested in only one spe-cific county or township, you may not need a publication that covers a much larger area.

How often does the publication come out? Foreclosure auction lists can come out weekly, biweekly, and even monthly. My preference is for lists that come out weekly. The idea is to get the listings that give you the most lead time before the auctions begin, to complete your prebid preparations.

Do the publishers offer support services and advice if you are a subscriber? This service can be extremely valuable for inexperienced foreclosure

Figure 2-4. A sample legal
notice from a newspaper.

purchasers and might make the difference in your choice of one publication over another.

What is the publisher's fee, and does it offer discounted rates if you subscribe for longer periods? Some publishers will charge you a lower price if you subscribe to their publication for a longer term (that is, for six months rather than three months, or for one year rather than six months, and so forth). Also, ask whether the fee is discounted if you subscribe to more than one county or township.

Announcements in Local Newspapers

Pursuant to state laws, a foreclosing lender may be required to publicize an upcoming auction. You may be able to find this information in the legal notices section of your local newspaper. Figure 2-4 is an illustration of a sample legal notice. The legal notice usually includes the name of the foreclosing lender, the defaulting borrower(s), the index number that the foreclosing lender's attorney or trustee purchased when the action was filed, the legal description of the property, and other information required by the foreclosure statutes in your state.

3

The Basics of Buying Foreclosures after the Auction—from Banks

The second opportunity to purchase foreclosures is after the auction, when banks—also referred to throughout this book as lending institutions—(Chapter 3) and government agencies (Chapter 4) sell repossessed foreclosed properties from their inventories.

In Chapter 3, we look at how properties become part of a bank's inventory, why banks are so highly motivated to sell these properties, and the step-by-step negotiating strategies that help you cut through the red tape and rise above your competition. Sources of bank foreclosure lists are detailed to help you get started. Finally, to give you a more global perspective, buying foreclosures from a bank's inventory is compared and contrasted with buying foreclosures at bank auctions.

Defining Bank-Owned Properties

There are two basic ways in which a property becomes bank-owned: (1) the property was not sold at the public auction, or (2) the deed to the property was turned over to the lender by the owners as an alternative to foreclosure.

The Property Was Not Sold at the Public Auction

Sometimes nobody shows up to bid on a property that is being sold at a foreclosure auction. Here are some of the most common reasons for this outcome.

Perhaps the opening bid amount exceeded the public's perceived value of the property, and therefore people did not consider it to be a good buy. For example, if the liens, judgments, legal fees, and other costs bring the upset price of a property up to $325,000, and the market value is only $300,000, then this would obviously not be a property to bid on.

Another reason why a property was not sold at an auction is that a forecast of severe storms and/or other potentially dangerous weather conditions kept bidders from attending.

Yet another reason why a property was not sold is that it was not publicized properly and the bidding public was unaware of the date and/or time and/or location of the auction.

When a property is not sold at the auction, the bank "buys it back" for the upset price, and it becomes part of the bank's inventory.

The Deed to the Property Was Returned to the Lender (a.k.a. a "Friendly" Foreclosure)

Sometimes a property never reaches the auction because the owner, who is experiencing (or anticipating) severe financial hardship, works out an agreement with the lender to turn over the deed (and the keys) in exchange for a full release from the remaining mortgage obligation. This procedure is called giving "a deed in lieu of foreclosure." It is also known as a friendly foreclosure. While lenders are not obligated to accept a deed in lieu of foreclosure, if the value of the property is equal to the outstanding mortgage balance, it makes sense for the lender to bypass the unnecessary expense and time that will be expended to initiate the procedure. The defaulting borrower benefits by minimizing the damage to his or her credit rating and eliminating the risk of a deficiency judgment if the auction fails to produce enough money to cover the outstanding mortgage balance. (Please note that deficiency judgments may not apply in trust deed states.)

There is also, however, a downside to this strategy for the defaulting borrower: if the property sells for more than the outstanding mortgage balance, the defaulting borrower forfeits the right to receive any overage (also known as surplus); instead, it goes to the lender that accepted the deed in lieu of foreclosure.

Redefining Bank-Owned Properties

If a property is not sold at the auction or if the lender accepts the deed in lieu of foreclosure, the lender takes title to the property, and the property becomes part of the lender's inventory. Some lenders call the properties in their inventories "REOs" (Real Estate Owned), others call them "OREs" (Owned Real Estate), and some lenders simply call them "bank-owned real estate."*

---

* In this book, the terms *lender* and *bank* are used interchangeably.

A Lender's View of
Bank-Owned Property

The foreclosure stigma that conjured up an image of an evil banker with a black cape, moustache, and top hat is a long-forgotten memory. Lending institutions have become reluctant property owners, charged with the overwhelming task of managing, marketing, and selling the repossessed properties in their inventories. Here are five reasons why foreclosures are a lender's nightmare.

Problem 1: property damage. If the house is vacant, it is sitting in the bank's inventory waiting to be vandalized. In areas with colder climates, the winter months pose an additional threat of frozen pipes unless the property is "winterized"—another expense. And we all know how quickly word gets around when there is a vacant house in the neighborhood. The property could easily become a hangout for local teenagers and a target for break-ins.

Problem 2: overhead expenses. The lender is responsible for paying the monthly expenses for the upkeep and maintenance of each property in its inventory until the property is sold. These expenses include homeowner's insurance (to cover the risk of fire damage and other property-related claims), liability insurance (to protect the bank if someone is hurt on the premises), property taxes, lawn care, snow removal, real estate appraisal fees (for estimates of market value), and real estate broker fees (for managing and selling the property)—to name just a few. To provide a context here, one REO specialist for a major lender told me that it cost $1 million per month to cover the expenses for the 500 properties in his inventory!

Problem 3: money must be held in reserve to cover nonperforming assets. When a borrower defaults on a loan secured by a mortgage or deed of trust, the foreclosing lender considers the property to be a "nonperforming asset." Federal banking regulations require banks to hold money in reserve to cover the expenses for the nonperforming assets in their inventories. (Personally, I've always thought that these properties should be called "nonperforming liabilities" because of the losses that the lender incurs.) Banks conduct business by charging interest on money they lend out. However, if they are unable to make loans because their funds must be held in reserve to cover their nonperforming assets, lenders cannot conduct business. Thus, lenders are highly motivated to sell the properties quickly.

So, to attract buyers, why don't lenders advertise lists of their REO addresses in the major newspapers? They could even implement promotional events and use catchy marketing headlines. For example:

> **Overstocked—Must Sell Our Inventory to Make Room for New Properties**

Or how about:

> **Year-End Clearance—Buy Two Foreclosures and Get the Third One for Half Price**

The answer is that the lending institutions are stuck in a "catch-22" situation. Here's why.

Problem 4: advertising a supply of foreclosures would be harmful to the lender's public image. If a lender listed the addresses of the foreclosed properties in its inventory, people would never want to apply to that lender for a loan. They would be afraid that the lender would publicize their addresses if they fell behind in their payments, and they wouldn't want all their friends to know that they were having financial problems. Furthermore, a large inventory of foreclosures could make the lender's financial position appear shaky, and people might hesitate to deposit their money in a savings account with a lender that appears to be unstable.

The lenders are better off bypassing the newspaper advertising campaign. But wait a minute! As long as they have to get rid of the properties quickly, why not just sell them for 50 cents on the dollar?

This brings us to Problem 5.

Problem 5: federal regulations prohibit "dumping" in a neighborhood. It is well established that the appraised values of properties in a local marketplace are determined by the sales prices of similar properties nearby that were sold recently. Consequently, selling foreclosures for pennies on the dollar (a.k.a. "dumping" the properties by selling them for a below-market price) would have a negative impact on the value of the other homes in that area.

Solution. The best solution—and the one that lenders have used and continue to use successfully—is to offer incredibly favorable financing terms to attract people who wish to buy foreclosures from the lenders' inventories. The result is deeply discounted interest rates and points, reductions in closing costs, and other loan features that borrowers can't find anywhere else.

An REO Purchase versus a Bank Auction Purchase

The differences between purchasing a foreclosure property at a bank auction and purchasing a bank-owned property from the bank's inventory can vary from lender to lender and from state to state.

Clear title. If you purchase a property at an auction, you may be responsible for unexpected liens and judgments (see Chapter 2). By contrast, most bank-owned properties are sold with clear title. The lending institution usually satisfies any outstanding liens and judgments when it takes the property into its inventory.

The asking price. The manner in which the asking price is established is another factor that distinguishes an auction foreclosure from a bank-owned foreclosure. While property that is sold at a bank auction can have an upset price that is less than market value because the price is set at the unpaid mortgage balance plus the back taxes and interest, legal fees, late charges, and other costs associated with the foreclosure proceeding, a lending institution will base the asking price of bank-owned property on market value. To illustrate this concept, if the market value of a property is $300,000 and the unpaid mortgage balance plus accumulated charges total $280,000, the opening bid amount at the auction would be $280,000. On the other hand, if the property is not sold at the auction and the lender has to take it back into its inventory and sell it as an REO, the asking price of the property would be set at the market value price of $300,000.

Evicting the occupants. If you purchase a property at a foreclosure auction, you are responsible for evicting any occupants after you become the new owner. Conversely, the REO seller may have evicted the occupants from its bank-owned property, thereby eliminating the time and expense of eviction procedures.

Presenting your offer. When you purchase a property at a foreclosure auction, the offers are usually communicated through the process of oral bidding. By contrast, offers for a bank-owned property are usually submitted in writing to the lender (or to the lender's asset manager or real estate broker).

Seller financing. When you purchase a property at a bank auction, the referee, sheriff, or trustee does not provide financing—you pay for the property with cash or you arrange for financing independently through a lending institution. In comparison, when you purchase a bank-owned property, you can usually negotiate attractive financing terms with the lending institution that owns the property and also happens to be the seller. Remember that the upkeep of bank-owned property costs a lot of money, and it is beneficial for bank-owned property sellers to offer favorable financing terms as an incentive to sell the property quickly.

"As-is" condition.   Unlike at a foreclosure auction, where properties are purchased in "as-is" condition, when you purchase a bank-owned property from a lending institution, the lending institution may agree to give you credit toward making necessary structural repairs. This is because a bank does not want the negative publicity that could result if, for example, someone who had purchased a foreclosure from XXX Bank the previous week was seriously hurt when the cesspool caved in.

Figure 3-1 compares and contrasts the basic distinctions between purchasing a foreclosure at a bank auction and purchasing an REO from a bank's inventory.

Finding REOs

Lending Institutions

Years ago, lending institutions would not admit that they had foreclosed properties in their inventories. As we discussed earlier in this chapter, it could hurt a lender's public image if potential borrowers were to think that the lending institution would take drastic action (such as foreclosing) if borrowers didn't pay their home loans. Today, however, because of the vast numbers of properties in their inventories, many lending institutions have "come out of the closet" and are willing to admit openly that they have bank-owned foreclosures available for sale. Some lenders even prepare lists of their bank-owned properties with attractive financing terms to make the properties easier to buy.

You can contact lenders and ask for their foreclosure department or their asset-recovery division, asset liquidation department, REO or ORE department, or whatever department is in charge of bank-owned property. Ask for a list of the lenders' available properties and information about the procedures you must follow in order to purchase these properties.

Web Sites

Most lending institutions use Web sites to advertise the services they provide for their customers, and you may find information about

BUYING A FORECLOSURE AT A BANK AUCTION VERSUS BUYING AN REO FROM A BANK OR GOVERNMENT AGENCY'S INVENTORY

BUYING A FORECLOSURE AT A BANK AUCTION	BUYING AN REO FROM A BANK OR GOVERNMENT AGENCY'S INVENTORY
1. The asking price is based on the unpaid loan balance plus expenses.	1. The asking price is based on market value.
2. The contract terms do not include a "financing contingency clause" (a.k.a. "mortgage contingency clause").	2. The REO contract usually includes a financing (a.k.a. mortgage) contingency clause, and the REO seller may also provide financing terms that are extremely favorable to a buyer.
3. The burden of evicting the current occupants is on the new owner, after the property is conveyed.	3. The REO seller may already have evicted the occupants before the property was placed on the market.
4. The plumbing, heating, and electrical systems and the appliances and roof are sold in "as-is" condition.	4. The REO seller may agree to pay for repairs if structural damage is discovered.
5. The defaulting borrower's right of redemption may extend beyond the auction date.	5. The REO seller has no right of redemption after the property is conveyed to the new owner.
6. The new owner may be responsible for liens and judgments in addition to the purchase price.	6. The REO seller usually clears up any existing title problems (i.e., liens and judgments on the premises) before the property is conveyed to the new owner.
7. The manner of making an offer to purchase the property is by oral bidding at a public foreclosure auction.	7. The manner of making an offer to purchase the property is by written offer to the REO seller or the REO seller's agent.

Figure 3-1. Buying a foreclosure at a bank auction vs. buying an REO from a bank or government agency's inventory.

foreclosures posted there. The information generally includes the property addresses, the asking prices, access to the properties, pictures of the properties, information about the property taxes, lot sizes, and contact information for access to the properties.

Real Estate Offices

Another source of foreclosure listings is local real estate companies. Most lending institutions do not have the property management capabilities or the staffing to manage, repair, advertise, and show the properties in their inventories to buyers. After all, banks are not in the business of selling real estate; their function is to lend money to people who want to buy real estate. As a result, in many cases, lending institutions give listings of their bank-owned properties to local real estate brokers. The real estate professionals advertise the properties, show them to prospective buyers, and present offers to the lender; if the property is sold, the lender pays the broker's fee.

Word of Mouth/Observation

One more very viable source of REO properties is through the grapevine—from friends, family, or acquaintances who know someone who was foreclosed on by a bank, or who know of a house in their neighborhood that was recently boarded up by a bank. In some cases, you may coincidentally come upon a bank-owned property while you are driving around in a town where you would like to own a home. In those cases, a sign may have been posted with the name of the bank that owns the property and a telephone number to contact for more information. If no sign is posted, the next-door neighbors are good sources of information and can usually tell you something that can help you find the owner. I have also identified unknown REO owners by researching the records at the property tax collection office that services the area where the property is situated. The entity that is paying the property taxes is usually the REO owner (or its respresentative).

Preparing Your Offer

More often than not, the list from the lending institution that is selling the property includes the asking price. You should not assume that this price is set in stone. When you are ready to make your offer, you will do so based on the price that is best for you. (Inspection techniques are covered in Chapter 9, and instructions for preparing a bid sheet to establish your purchase offer can be found in Chapter 10.) Remember two important things:

1. The properties are sitting in the lender's inventory, costing the bank money.
2. The lender is a highly motivated seller.

The offer you make should be in writing, and it should be as specific as possible. Here are the most important items to include:

The address.   Clearly indicate the exact address of the property you wish to purchase. The lending institution may have assigned identification numbers to the properties in its inventory, and, if so, you should include the number of the property you are interested in as well.

The purchase price.   Your offer should include the purchase price, that is, the amount of money you are offering to pay for the property.

The deposit.   Some lending institutions may require you to send in a deposit (also called a *binder*) along with your offer. The deposit is usually a nominal amount ($100) that will be refunded or returned to you if your offer is not accepted. If your offer is accepted, the lending institution keeps your deposit and applies it to the purchase price.

The financing terms.   If you want the lender to provide you with financing for the property, your offer should include the financing terms, including the interest rate you wish to pay, the amount you want to borrow, and the length of time it will take to repay the mortgage (usually 15, 20, or 30 years).

The down payment.   The difference between the purchase price and the amount a lending institution will allow you to borrow is called the *down payment.* Your offer should specify the total down payment amount as well as its allocation, in other words, how much of that amount you wish to pay at the time you sign the sales contract and how much will be paid at closing. For example, you are offering to purchase the REO for $200,000. You are obtaining 90 percent financing ($180,000), either from the REO seller or another lender. You will pay 10 percent of the purchase price ($20,000) as a down payment allocated as follows: 5 percent ($10,000) at the time you sign the sales contract and the remaining 5 percent ($10,000) on the day of the closing when you become the new owner.

The closing date.   Your offer should stipulate the day on which you wish to take title (ownership) and possession.

Your contact information.   Be certain to have your name, address, and telephone number on the letter so that a representative from the lending institution can contact you with a decision regarding your offer.

Figure 3-2 is an example of an offer letter for a bank-owned property.

Offer Letter for a Bank-Owned Property

Today's Date:

XYZ Bank
000 Smith Street
Anytown, U.S.A. 00000

Attn: Foreclosure Department

Dear _____ :

With reference to the property located at _____,
I would like to submit the following offer:

    Purchase price:

    Down payment:

    Financing terms:

    Closing date:

    Amount enclosed (deposit/binder):

Please contact me at your earliest convenience with your acceptance.

The best time to contact me is between _____and _____.

My telephone number is: (____) _____ .

My current address is:

Very truly yours,

(Your Name)

Figure 3-2. An example of an offer letter for a bank-owned property.

Negotiating Strategies That Help You Cut through the Red Tape

Justify Low Offers with Documentation

Keep in mind that in order to comply with banking laws, lending institutions must price bank-owned properties at market value to prevent the negative impact that underpricing would have on the values of other properties in the neighborhood. There are, however, extenuating circumstances—specifically, the substandard condition of a property—that legitimately affect the market value and, as a result, justify a deeply discounted sales price.

It is possible that, in some cases, a property is priced at a ridiculously high amount. This could just be a mistake on the part of the appraiser or another explanation is that the appraisal was initially prepared a while ago, when the property first went into the bank's inventory at which time it _had_ a kitchen. Since then, the property may have been vandalized, and, as a result, the value has been substantially reduced. If you want to purchase the property, don't just send in a low offer with a note stating that the amount you are offering to pay is low because "the property needs a lot of work." Instead, take pictures of the vandalized rooms to accurately illustrate its present condition (e.g., the fact that most of the kitchen has been gutted), and send the pictures with estimates from two contractors along with your offer. By doing so, you are helping the lender justify its decision to accept an offer that is lower than what it previously listed as the property's market value.

Rise above Your Competition

There are likely to be several people submitting offers simultaneously for the same property that you are interested in. What do you have that would be highly regarded by a lender, and that would give you an edge over your competitors if their offers are for similar amounts? The answer is, an outstanding credit report.

First, if you have excellent credit, there is a greater likelihood that you will be able to obtain financing, either from the lender that is selling this property or from another financial institution, without the customary delays that can accompany a questionable credit history. This will help expedite the sales process.

Second, an outstanding credit rating is indicative of your willingness and ability to make your mortgage payments in a timely fashion, which means that if your offer is accepted, the owner of the bank-owned property doesn't have to worry that the property will return to its inventory in the near future.

You can call and inquire as to which of the credit report providers the lender prefers. Obtain a copy of your credit report from the reporting agency (or agencies) and submit it along with your written offer. Your diligence in maintaining a great credit rating is something to be proud of, and it makes good business sense to use this hard-earned resource to your advantage.

4

The Basics of Buying Foreclosures after the Auction—from Federal, State, and Local Government Agencies

In Chapter 3, we looked at buying bank-owned foreclosures after the auction. We expand on this multifaceted opportunity in Chapter 4 as we tap into another source of repossessed properties—federal, state, and local government agencies. The manner in which a property becomes part of each government agency's inventory is also included for general background information.

Defining Government-Owned Property

Federal, state, and local governments have a variety of residential, commercial, and industrial foreclosed properties in their inventories as well as vacant land. Each agency's specifications for bidders to inspect these properties and submit offers to purchase them are clearly detailed in government pamphlets, on government Web sites, and in bidding packages that government agency representatives send out to people who request them. In most cases, the lists include the asking price, but as noted in Chapter 3, when you are ready to make your offer, you will do so based on the price that is best for you. In Chapter 9, we cover inspection techniques that apply to all types of foreclosures, and in Chapter 10, we review instructions for preparing a bid sheet.

The rest of this chapter details the names and contact information for the government agencies.

Finding Government-Owned Foreclosures

Government Services Administration (GSA) Sales

The Government Services Administration (GSA) Property Disposition Offices oversee the sale of real estate that was formerly used by the federal government. The list includes office buildings, vacant land, high-rise buildings, residential homes previously occupied by military families, and residential property that has been confiscated by law enforcement officials.

The U.S. government offers these surplus properties to the general public through a system of public bidding in order to increase its revenues. An invitation for bids (IFB) is prepared for each property that is sold. The IFB includes directions to the property and instructions on whom to contact to inspect the property prior to bidding.

Telephone contact: To find out about upcoming sales, contact your local General Services Administration office and ask for the U.S. Real Property Sales List.

Internet (www) contact: You can access the U.S. Real Property Sales List and the GSA Official Bid Forms through the Property Disposal Web page on the GSA.gov Web site.

Department of Housing and Urban Development (HUD) Sales (a.k.a. FHA Foreclosures)

U.S. Department of Housing and Urban Development (HUD) sales, also known as Federal Housing Administration (FHA) foreclosures, occur when a borrower defaults and the lender forecloses on an FHA loan. HUD pays the lending institution for the outstanding loan and the expenses incurred. HUD then takes ownership of the property and resells it to the public.

HUD guidelines require buyers to go through HUD's designated real estate brokers in order to inspect and bid on the foreclosures that HUD sells. HUD provides buyers with a list of designated brokers to contact for information about properties they are interested in purchasing. The HUD area broker prepares the buyers' bids and submits them to HUD. Sealed bids are accepted by mail and must include a 10 percent down payment. HUD will pay the real estate broker's commission if the offer is accepted.

In many cases, HUD will provide lower-interest mortgages for these properties, but purchasers may be required to live in the house and not sell it or rent it out to others for a specified period (e.g., three years).

Newspaper: HUD often posts upcoming auction information in local newspapers on a weekly basis. Figure 4-1 is an illustration of a HUD advertisement.

Telephone contact: To find out more about upcoming HUD/FHA sales and the designated HUD brokers in your area, contact your local HUD office.

U.S. DEPARTMENT OF HOUSING & URBAN DEVELOPMENT
26 Federal Plaza, New York, N.Y. 10278-0068

- Purchasers must obtain their own financing for all sales.

- Please contact a HUD-registered real estate broker of your choice to see or bid on any properties listed.

- These properties may contain code violations.

- HUD reserves the right to reject any or all bids and to waive any informality or irregularity in any bids.

- An earnest money deposit equaling 5 percent of the list price, not to exceed $2,000, but no less than $500 is required with each offer to purchase. Earnest money deposits on vacant land require 10% of the list price.

- Deposits are to be by certified cashier's check or money order only, made payable to HUD.

- Properties subject to prior sale, omissions, errors, change in price or withdrawal without notice.

Bid Due Date: Bids Opened:

NOT ELIGIBLE FOR MORTGAGE INSURANCE

AS-IS ALL CASH

CASE #	ADDRESS	MIM BID PRICE	BED	BATHS

NEW LISTINGS

BRONX

| 373-088103-203ND | Morris Avenue Bronx, NY 10456 | $20,000.00 | 9 | 3 |

SUFFOLK

| 373-194811-321ND | Wilson Avenue Central Islip, NY 11722 | $65,000.00 | 3 | 2 |

NASSAU

| 374-142033-203ND * | Shonnard Avenue Freeport, NY 11520 | $79,990.00 | 3 | 2 |

*(Note: Earnest Money Deposit required for this property is $3,995.00)

HAND DELIVERED TO:
PROPERTY DISPOSITION ROOM 3237
26 FEDERAL PLAZA, NEW YORK, NY 10278

Figure 4-1. An illustration of an HUD advertisement.

Internet (www) contact: You can access HUD homes on the Surplus/ Excess Properties Web page on the Department of Housing and Urban Development.gov Web site.

Department of Veterans Affairs (DVA) Sales

Department of Veterans Affairs sales occur when the Department of Veterans Affairs (DVA) repossesses property from a serviceman or servicewoman who has been foreclosed on. You are not required to be a serviceperson or even an owner-occupant (someone who will buy the property to live in and not lease it to others as a rental property) to purchase these properties. The DVA utilizes the services of local real estate brokers to sell the properties to the public. The brokers are responsible for showing the properties to prospective buyers and preparing purchase offers. The DVA pays the broker's commission.

The DVA offers favorable financing terms for many DVA-owned properties. Successful high bidders must satisfy steady employment and good credit criteria.

Telephone contact: To find out more about DVA-owned foreclosures, call your local Department of Veterans Affairs office and ask for information about the Home Loan Guaranty Services.

Internet (www) contact: You can access DVA-owned foreclosures on the Home Loan Guaranty Services Web page on the Department of Veterans Affairs.gov Web site.

Federal Deposit Insurance Corporation (FDIC) Sales

The Federal Deposit Insurance Corporation is an independent agency of the U.S. government. While it is best known as the provider of the insurance that protects savings and checking account deposits in U.S. banks, the FDIC also functions in the role of its predecessor, the Resolution Trust Corporation, as the receiver when an insured financial institution fails.

In its role as receiver, the FDIC either pays the insured deposits directly to the customers of the failed institution or transfers the deposits to another financial institution, where depositors can gain immediate access to their funds.

In its role as a government-owned foreclosure seller, the FDIC provides lists of properties from its inventory to purchasers who are interested in buying residential and commercial property and vacant land.

Telephone contact: To find out more about FDIC-owned foreclosures, call your local FDIC office and ask for information about Real Estate Property for Sale.

Internet (www) contact: You can access FDIC-owned foreclosures on the Buying from and Selling to the FDIC Web page on the FDIC.gov Web site.

Federal Home Loan Mortgage Corporation (Freddie Mac) Sales

The Federal Home Loan Mortgage Corporation (Freddie Mac) is a publicly chartered agency that buys residential mortgages from lending institutions. Freddie Mac sells its foreclosures through real estate brokers who manage the properties in each state. Freddie Mac prefers selling to owner-occupants but also works with investors. HomeSteps Asset Services is the unit that markets foreclosed homes for Freddie Mac and provides special financing for qualified purchasers of Freddie Mac–owned properties.

Telephone contact: To find out more about Freddie Mac–owned foreclosures, call your local Freddie Mac office and ask for information about HomeSteps Foreclosure Listings.

Internet (www) contact: You can access Freddie Mac–owned foreclosures on the HomeSteps.com Web site.

Federal National Mortgage Association (Fannie Mae) Sales

The Federal National Mortgage Association (Fannie Mae) is the largest purchaser of mortgages in the secondary market. Fannie Mae offers financing incentives to qualified buyers through its staff of HomePath specialists. Fannie Mae hires real estate brokers to sell the foreclosures in its inventory. A list of Fannie Mae–owned foreclosures with property information and the names and contact information for the real estate brokers is available by telephone and on the Internet.

Telephone contact: To find out more about Fannie Mae–owned property, call your local Fannie Mae Public Information Office and ask for information about foreclosure listings.

Internet (www) contact: You can access Fannie Mae foreclosures on the agency's Web site at Fanniemae.com.

State/County/Town Government Agencies

Local (state, county, and town) government agencies that provide services to their communities may also be sources of surplus foreclosures.

These agencies may include, but are certainly not limited to, departments of transportation, departments of social services, housing authorities, property tax agencies, and homeowners associations.

5

The Basics of Buying Foreclosures before the Auction

Defaulting borrowers benefit from pre-auction purchases because they can preserve their credit ratings and avoid the risk of incurring additional debt.* Buyers benefit from pre-auction purchases because they can buy a property before the costs associated with foreclosure proceedings drive up the purchase price.

In Chapter 5, we explore the third opportunity to purchase foreclosures, where buyers help defaulting borrowers avoid foreclosure by purchasing property directly from them before the auction commences.

---

* In this chapter, *defaulting borrowers* and *defaulting owners* are people who have fallen behsind in paying their loans; they may be anywhere from one day late up to the date the auction is scheduled to occur.

Understanding the Defaulting Owners

Before you start to knock on the doors of people who are facing fore-closure, it is important that you understand the psychological effect that the pending foreclosure may be having on them. It is also good to know the other alternatives that are available to them, the viability of those options, and the time frame within which decisions must be made so that you can accurately organize your plan of action.

As a purchaser of foreclosures for myself and for other investors, and as an attorney, I've worked with a lot of people who were trying to sell their homes to avoid foreclosure. In response to my questions as to what caused them to fall so far behind in making their loan payments, some people said that injuries or illnesses had caused them to lose a lot of time from work, and some others had been laid off. In many cases, divorce had taken its toll. Some people had taken an equity loan to start a business that failed, and that extra monetary obligation each month was choking them. But by far, the most prevalent causes were denial and procrastination. People just didn't believe it could happen to them. They "put their heads in the sand," ignored any attempts by the lenders to try to remedy the situation, and figured that somehow, somewhere, someone would bail them out before they lost their homes.

How You Can Help

If you feel uncomfortable about contacting people who are being fore-closed on, it may help you to know that you may be their last (and best) alternative to the menacing threat of foreclosure, which is, in most cases, inevitable. For many defaulting borrowers, the property has become an albatross, a heavy burden that they can't afford to keep and are unable to sell.

If you can negotiate an agreement to purchase the property and the transaction takes place before the lender sells it at a foreclosure auc-tion, there are several important ways in which you can change these borrowers' lives.

First, you can help them save some equity, so that they don't lose everything. Depending on the condition of the property and general market conditions, if you are paying them even a small amount of money above their loan balance, it may be more than they would have ended up with if the property went to auction.

Second, you can help them save their credit. If the property is sold before the auction is held, the defaulting owners' credit reports will show late loan payments, but will not reflect the stigma of a foreclosure sale (the effects of which can damage their credit rating for years to come). This is a very valuable result, especially if the defaulting owners would like to relocate to a more affordable area, with a lower cost of living, and buy another home there in the near future.

Third, you can help them avoid losing future income. If the property ends up in foreclosure and it is not sold at the auction, it becomes a bank-owned property in the lender's inventory. If it is subsequently sold for less than the amount that was owed, the foreclosing lender can file a deficiency judgment against the defaulting owners for the difference. For example, let's say that two borrowers (husband and wife) fall behind on their loan payments and the lender brings a foreclosure action. If the upset price for the defaulting owners' house (including legal fees, back interest, late charges, and other costs associated with the foreclosure proceeding) totals $200,000 and the house is subse-quently sold for $140,000, the foreclosing lender can file a deficiency judgment against the defaulting borrowers for the $60,000 difference. A deficiency judgment can result in garnished wages, and, depending on state law, if the defaulting borrowers have other assets, those assets can be seized and sold to pay off the outstanding balance owed to the foreclosing lender. Exceptions may apply for borrowers in some cir-cumstances, including insolvency (as defined by your income tax authority) and/or bankruptcy.

Uncle Sam to the Rescue!

On December 20, 2007, the Mortgage Debt Cancellation Relief Act was enacted in response to the subprime crisis, declining property values, and the alarming number of foreclosures nationwide. Before this new law was enacted, when any part of mortgage debt was forgiven or discharged, the borrower was taxed on this "phantom income" at his or her ordinary income rates. The consequences for the defaulting borrowers were devastating. Not only did they lose their home, but now they also owed federal income taxes and, if applicable, state, city, and other local income taxes as well on the forgiven debt, even though they never received any cash. This new law applies to mortgage debt on the borrowers' principal residence that is forgiven or discharged in a short sale, a workout agreement with a lender, or a foreclosure during the time period from January 1, 2007, through December 31, 2009. Borrowers who qualify will not be required to pay income taxes on the forgiven or discharged amount. If you are negotiating a foreclosure transaction with defaulting borrowers, they should contact a tax advisor or CPA to find out if they qualify for the forgiven debt exclusion under this new Act.

Negotiating with Defaulting Owners—When the Property Has Equity

Before you try to buy a property from defaulting owners, it is helpful to be aware of some of the other options available to them for avoiding foreclosure and to have some insight concerning which of these options may or may not be viable. In the following situations, if defaulting owners reject your offer to purchase the property from them initially, your best negotiating strategy may simply be to give them your contact number so that they can reach you if the other options they are relying on to avoid foreclosure cannot be brought to fruition.

Option 1: They can sell the property on the open market. Quite often, the defaulting owners are trying to sell the house to avoid foreclosure, but they have it listed for sale at too high a price, even though they risk losing everything if they can't sell it before the lender forecloses.

If the defaulting owners are not responsive and resist your attempts to talk to them about selling to you, just give them your business card, or write your name and contact number on a piece of paper for them. Touch base with them periodically (i.e., every other week or so) to ask if they have been successful in their attempts to sell the house. Remember that the defaulting owners still own the property up until the auction begins. This means that they still have the right to avoid foreclosure by selling the property (hopefully, to you) before the auction commences.

Option 2: They can file for bankruptcy. Another way in which people can save their homes from foreclosure is to file for bankruptcy. What these people may not know is that borrowers who file for bankruptcy are still responsible for paying the loan each month; if they do not do so, the property will be released from the protection of the bankruptcy court and can be sold by the lender at a foreclosure auction. Also, some forms of bankruptcy require a reorganization plan for debt consolidation and repayment, and the plan may be turned down by the courts if the people lack sufficient income to repay those debts in accordance with the plan.

Option 3: They can apply for a "hard-money" loan. Some defaulting homeowners borrow money and use it to bring their monthly loan payments current. A hard-money loan is different from "break-your-arm" financing by a loan shark. Hard-money lenders traditionally charge much higher interest rates and a greater number of points than conventional lenders, and the borrowers must have a source of income in order to pay the loan back. This may, once again, pose a problem for borrowers whose delinquency is the result of a job loss.

Option 4: They can work out a payment plan with the lender. Another alternative available to the defaulting homeowner is to work out a payment plan with the foreclosing lender. But there is a possibility that the borrowers may already have defaulted on payment plans, and the foreclosing lender may not be willing to extend any more deadlines.

Option 5: They can give the foreclosing lender the "deed in lieu of foreclosure" and leave. As discussed in Chapter 3, the borrowers can ask the lender to accept the deed in lieu of foreclosure. If the lender agrees, the borrowers convey the deed and turn over the house keys to the lender to prevent the foreclosure sale, and the transaction is considered an even exchange. Be aware that this alternative may not be available if the lender does not agree to it. Also, be aware that once the property is accepted into the bank's inventory, if it subsequently sells for more money than the outstanding balance, the lender keeps the surplus money; the overage will not be credited back to the defaulting owners.

Negotiating with Defaulting Owners—When There Is Negative Equity (a.k.a. "Short Sales")

Sometimes the defaulting owners are unable to sell the property because, after the foreclosure has begun and legal fees, interest charges, and other such costs have been added to the unpaid loan balance, the owners would have to sell the property for more than it is worth in order to pay off the loan. That is, of course, assuming that they can sell the house privately before the lender forecloses. This situation most frequently occurs when the market values of real estate decline, especially when the property was highly leveraged to begin with (i.e., the buyers put down very little money as a down payment and took out a large loan). And if the inflated sales price doesn't make the property impossible to sell, the fact that it is probably in less than stellar condition (as a result of the owner's financial difficulties) will probably do the trick.

When the loan balance exceeds the value of the property, what many people don't realize is that lending institutions can, and, in many circumstances, do, agree to accept less than the outstanding loan balance as payment in full. This arrangement is called a *short sale* (because the proceeds of the property sale fall short of the amount needed to pay off the loan balance). It is also known as a *cram down* (because the lender crams down the outstanding balance of the loan so that it is in conformity with the real market value of the property).

Even though the property still legally belongs to the defaulting homeowner until the auction cuts off his or her interests, a short sale situation that arises where the defaulting owner agrees to sell the property for an amount less than the outstanding loan balance is the one circumstance in which the lender must be included in the sales negotiations. Because the lender is financially affected by the transaction, it has to be a part of the negotiations and must agree to the short sale.

Negotiating the Short Sale

The lender has a good reason to work with the defaulting owner in this circumstance. Accepting your lower offer may cost the lender a few thousand dollars now, but that initial "investment" will save the lender many thousands of dollars in the long run. Why? Because if you don't buy the property, it will be auctioned at a higher upset price (inflated by back taxes, legal fees, interest, and other such costs), and since that price exceeds market value, it is unlikely that anyone will buy it at the auction. The property will then become a nonperforming asset in the lender's portfolio, and the lender will incur all of the extra expenses for the upkeep and maintenance of the premises, including property insurance and liability coverage, property taxes, and so on. Finally, to add insult to injury, the lender will have to lower the asking price in order to sell the property for market value, and ultimately, at the end of the day, the amount that it will sell for will probably be equal to (or less than) what you originally offered.

Once the defaulting owners accept your offer, you may be able to negotiate with the foreclosing lender directly. This is especially true when the auction date is looming and time is of the essence, and when the defaulting owners are unsophisticated about the concept of short sales and intimidated by the prospect of trying to negotiate with the foreclosing lender on their own behalf. A word to the wise: I highly recommend that as part of the contract negotiations, the defaulting borrower should request confirmation in writing from the foreclosing lender that the short sale amount will be considered payment in full for the outstanding loan balance.

While each lender follows its own procedures for approving and processing transactions involving short sales, the basic process is similar for all lenders. The following information will help clarify many details; however, you will need to obtain more specific instructions from the defaulting borrower's lender.

New Legislation Affecting Short Sales

As discussed earlier in this chapter, the Mortgage Debt Cancellation Relief Act, adopted on December 20, 2007, relieves borrowers who are covered under the Act from paying income taxes on mortgage debt that is forgiven or discharged in a short sale, a foreclosure sale, or a workout with a lender during the period between January 1, 2007, and December 31, 2009. This legislation will play a huge role in helping defaulting borrowers to pay off their loans without the threat of being encumbered with federal and state income tax liens. Contact your financial/tax advisor for more information about how the Act applies in your specific circumstances.

The Parties Involved in a Short Sale

- The defaulting borrower, who wants to sell to avoid a foreclosure
- The prospective purchaser, who wants to buy the property at a fair price
- The foreclosing lender
- The foreclosing lender's loss mitigation department representative

The Objective

The defaulting borrower must convince the lender to accept less than the outstanding balance owed on the mortgage or deed of trust loan. To accomplish this, the loss mitigation department representative will require the defaulting borrower to prove that (1) the property's value has fallen below the outstanding loan balance, (2) the borrower is experiencing severe hardship and can no longer afford to pay the loan, and (3) if the property is sold, there is an actual, bona fide arm's-length transaction.

Proving the property value. The loss mitigation representative may ask the defaulting borrower to provide any or all of the following information:

- A recent appraisal of the property, along with pictures
- Listings of similar properties in the area that have sold recently
- Listings of similar properties in the area that are currently on the market
- An estimate for repairs that may be needed in order to sell the property

Proving hardship. The loss mitigation representative may require any or all of the following information from the defaulting borrower:

- A hardship letter signed by the defaulting borrower
- A proposed sales price for the lender to consider
- The lender's completed short sale application form
- A financial statement
- Two years of federal and state income tax returns or a letter of explanation stating why no tax returns were required to be filed
- Bank statements (covering six months to one year)
- Current pay stubs if the defaulting borrower is employed
- Credit reports from one or all of the consumer credit reporting agencies (Equifax, TransUnion, and Experian)
- Divorce decrees with child support/alimony obligations
- Releases from lienholders

Proving the sale. Instead of accepting a proposed sales price, the loss mitigation representative may require the defaulting borrower to sell the premises before the short sale can be considered. If so, here are the documents that may be required:

- A HUD 1 Settlement Statement.
- A copy of a fully executed sales contract.

- A seller's "net sheet"—a statement giving the proposed sales price minus expenses that will be deducted from the proceeds (e.g., property tax arrears, outstanding unpaid liens, attorney fees, real estate broker fees, and closing costs). After deducting the expenses, the net amount will be the remaining proceeds that will be available to pay off the foreclosing lender.

Additional requirements.   Government agencies that have insured or guaranteed the defaulting borrower's loan may have additional requirements that must be met before they will approve a short sale. These requirements may include owner-occupancy by the defaulting borrower, counseling by a HUD agency, limits on net sheet fixed expenses, and so on.

Steps in a Short Sale

1. Contact the lender for the name of the loss mitigation representative who will be initiating the short sale transaction.

2. The loss mitigation representative will require the defaulting owners to sign a form called a *waiver of confidentiality* (or its equivalent), which gives the foreclosing lender formal, written permission to discuss the transaction directly with the prospective purchaser or other third parties (e.g., a real estate broker who is involved with the sale, the defaulting borrower's attorney, and so on) in order to expedite the transaction.

3. The loss mitigation representative sends out the short sale package to the defaulting owner. The short sale package usually includes paperwork for the owner to fill out and return and instructions on how to fill out the documents.

4. The defaulting borrower obtains the required documents, fills out the forms, and returns the completed package to the loss mitigation representative.

5. The loss mitigation representative reviews the package and makes a determination based on the lender's guidelines.

6. The loss mitigation representative advises the defaulting borrower of the lender's approval or rejection of the short sale transaction.

Finding "Pre-Auction" Foreclosures

There are several sources that are available to you for finding people who are in default on their loans and thereby facing foreclosure.

Legal Notices in Local Newspapers

In many states, the foreclosure procedures require public notice prior to the auction. Upcoming auctions are frequently advertised by local custom (usually in the "legal notices" section in local newspapers).

Legal notices usually include the property address, the legal description of the property, and the date, time, and location of the auction. A sample legal notice can be found in Chapter 2, Figure 2-4.

Lis Pendens Lists

Banks will not publicize information about defaulting loans until the borrowers are in default and the foreclosure action commences. The manner in which the foreclosure action proceeds is usually guided by state statute, as discussed in Chapter 1. In states in which the foreclosure process is initiated by the filing of a notice of pending action (a.k.a. lis pendens) with the court, the documents are considered to be public notice, and they can be accessed at the county clerk's office in the county where the property is located.

There are also companies that sell lis pendens lists. You can look up the names of such companies on the Internet and in reference books in your local library. Sometimes the publishers of upcoming auction lists offer lis pendens lists as an additional accommodation to give their subscribers a chance to buy properties before as well as at an auction.

Local Real Estate Offices

When borrowers face severe enough financial difficulties that they must sell their homes quickly to avoid losing everything, they may reach out to a local real estate company for assistance. You can visit local real estate offices and ask the real estate professionals who work there to keep your name on file as someone who is interested in buying pre-auction properties.

Contacting Defaulting Owners

When you contact defaulting borrowers, be aware that they may still be in a state of denial and may not even wish to speak to you. If this happens, patient, compassionate persistence will be your key to success. Here are some techniques that can help you communicate and negotiate more effectively with defaulting owners.

Once Is Not Enough

It has been my experience that, in most cases, the typical defaulting borrowers will not show any interest in your offer to buy the property until the fourth time you contact them. Timing is everything. When the defaulting owners decide that it is time to act, you want to be the first person they turn to. For optimum results, call or send a letter (see page 69) approximately once every three weeks.

Dress for Success

If you are planning to meet with the defaulting borrowers face to face, please remember that you are dealing with people who are in financial peril. Should you wear your most expensive jewelry and your designer clothing, and have your airline ticket for a Hawaiian vacation strategically positioned (destination side pointed outward) in your pocket—you know, to assure them that you can afford to do business with them? Of course not! Because these people could be losing everything, it would be thoughtless and insensitive for you to flaunt your good fortune. It would also be a foolish business strategy because it almost begs the sellers to try to negotiate a higher purchase price from you, since you obviously can afford it. You are much better off wearing jeans or similarly suitable casual clothing. Above all, the most important things to bring with you are a friendly smile and a compassionate attitude.

Letters That Open Doors

If you feel uncomfortable about approaching the defaulting borrowers on a face-to-face basis initially, send them a letter instead. The letter itself can be typed or handwritten—the main criterion is legibility. If you have great handwriting, write out the letter; if your handwriting stinks (like mine does), type the letter. For a more personal approach, you should address the letter to the homeowners' names rather than to "Dear Occupant." The letter should indicate that you understand the problems the homeowners are having, that many, many people are in the same boat, and that they have nothing to be ashamed of. Keep the letter short, simple, and nonthreatening. An example of a letter to defaulting owners is illustrated in Figure 5-1.

Envelopes That Beg to Be Opened

While the most important hurdle for your letter is that the recipients can read what you wrote, the envelope faces a more daunting challenge: it must compel the recipients to open it up and read its contents.

An Example of a Letter to a Defaulting Borrower

Today's Date:

Defaulting Owners' Name(s)
000 Smith Street
Anytown, U.S.A. 00000

Dear _____:

I understand that you are having difficulty making your loan payments, as are many people in today's economy.

If you would be interested talking to me about a quick sale, please call me at (   )_____.

The best time to contact me is between the hours of _____ and _____.

Very truly yours,

(Your Name)

Figure 5-1. An example of a letter to a defaulting owner.

We don't want the defaulting owners to think that our letter is just another letter from a creditor who is threatening to sue them and, as a result, they throw the letter in the garbage without reading it. If that happens, they missed out on what could be their last chance to sell the property before the lender forecloses—simply because they didn't know they had another option.

You might begin with a handwritten, pastel-colored, "invitation-sized" envelope that cannot possibly be mistaken for a bill from a creditor. This way, it is more likely that the defaulting owners will read your letter. If they throw it in the garbage after they finish reading it, fine. At least they knew that there were other options available to them when they made their choice.

Remember, if you ever feel tacky or uncomfortable about approaching people who are experiencing financial difficulty, remind yourself that you can help them, but that they have to want to help themselves as well.

Additional Strategies and Tips for Buying Pre-Auction Foreclosures

Include These Contract Terms

If you are successful in reaching an agreement to buy a pre-auction property, your contract with the defaulting owners should be contingent upon the results of a title search. Your attorney can assist you in obtaining this. The search will confirm that there are no extra liens or judgments that you were unaware of and that, as the new owner, you could be responsible for. Do not release any money to the defaulting owners until your attorney reviews the title report and assures you that there are no problems.

Other contract terms include the repairs to the premises, if any, that the defaulting homeowner will complete prior to closing and the appliances, furnishings, and fixtures (e.g., window treatments, air conditioners, or carpeting) that are included in the sale of the property to you.

Use the "B" (as in Bankruptcy) Word in Self-Defense if the Lender Is Unreasonable

When a lender begins a foreclosure action, the defaulting owner often tries to sell the property to avoid losing his credit, his equity, and even his future earnings. And in most cases, a bona fide contract with a purchaser, along with a lender's commitment to finance the premises, is enough of a good-faith effort for a foreclosing lender to agree to postpone the auction for a reasonable period of time—that is, one or two weeks.

Sometimes, however, the foreclosing lender refuses to postpone the auction, and the sale cannot take place before the auction is held. The alternative for many defaulting owners in this situation is to file for bankruptcy, which temporarily stops the foreclosure from proceeding any further. Sometimes just advising the foreclosing lender that the defaulting owners intend to file for bankruptcy is enough to achieve the intended result—the foreclosing lender's cooperation in rescheduling the auction to a later date.

There are, however, very serious consequences to be aware of when people choose bankruptcy as an alternative to foreclosure. First, people with a bankruptcy in their credit history can expect to pay higher interest rates on future loans, and there is a strong likelihood that they will even be denied loans until the bankruptcy is discharged and/or they have established new credit. Second, laws that prohibit deed transfers by people who have filed for bankruptcy may cause problems for people who wish to convey the property. The defaulting owner may even be charged additional legal fees to release the property from bankruptcy protection so that it can be sold. Before choosing bankruptcy, defaulting owners should ask their attorneys if there is another remedy besides bankruptcy that allows them to delay the upcoming foreclosure auction so that they can sell the property.

On the other hand, if the defaulting owners are planning to move to another locale where the cost of living is more affordable for them and they intend to purchase another home shortly, foreclosure could be even more prejudicial than bankruptcy—especially to a prospective lender who does not want to see a foreclosure history repeat itself at her bank's expense.

Before making any final decisions, it is important for the defaulting owners to seek legal and financial advice regarding bankruptcy and foreclosure options based on their particular circumstances.

Buyers Beware: Has Your State Adopted a Home Equity Theft Prevention Act?

Many states have enacted statutes to protect defaulting borrowers from unscrupulous "scam artists" who use high-pressure techniques to trick them into signing away the title to their homes. The scam artist offers to refinance the house, pay off the loan, rescue the house from foreclosure, and then "reconvey" (resell) the house to the borrower after a given period of time (usually a year). The scam artist takes ownership of the house and fails to make payments on the new loan. The new lender forecloses, and, instead of being able to buy back the house, the duped homeowners are evicted by the next high bidders when the house is resold at another foreclosure auction.

Most home equity theft prevention statutes target sales to investors and give defaulting borrowers who own and occupy their one- to four-family homes the right to cancel or rescind a contract within a statutory number of days after the contract was signed; in some states, the deed to the property may also be rescinded within a statutory number of years. Most statutes mandate that sales agreements include written notice of the homeowner's right to cancel, and violators may be subject to civil fines and criminal charges. Furthermore, if your state has enacted a home equity sales statute, most sales contracts with terms that call for investors to reconvey property to the previous owner will be subject to scrutiny and may be rejected as uninsurable by title insurance companies because of the likelihood that the title company could be held liable for paying any costs associated with restoring the property to the original defaulting borrower if that defaulting borrower asserted his or her right to bring an action to reclaim the premises in the future.

Clarifying Government "Acts" of Kindness

To help you understand the purpose and intent of the government "Acts" discussed in this chapter, Home Equity Theft Prevention Acts are usually adopted by a state to protect defaulting homeowners from losing their homes to unscrupulous scammers. By contrast, The Mortgage Debt Cancellation Act was adopted by the federal government to protect defaulting homeowners from losing their future income to federal, state, and local tax collection agencies (i.e., the Internal Revenue Service).

6

Financing Foreclosures with Traditional Real Estate Loans

Just as you will spend many hours of preparation choosing the property that is right for you, you should take an equal amount of time and care in choosing a loan that best meets your present financial circumstances and your future economic goals. To accomplish this, in Chapter 6 we look at the types of loans available in today's real estate market and the benefits and risks associated with each type of loan.

Please note that the numbers in Chapter 6 are for demonstration purposes only—in some parts of the country, housing prices for residential properties and rentals as well as housing costs, including property taxes and homeowner's insurance, are lower than the numbers set forth in this chapter, and in some parts of the country, the prices will be higher.

RIDDLE

What is the largest purchase most people make during their lifetimes?

A home?

No!

Guess again.

The answer is—a real estate loan.

Whether you are a first-time foreclosure purchaser or are purchasing your third foreclosure, a loan is the most popular way to finance foreclosures. Unfortunately, for people who are unfamiliar with the lending process, applying for a real estate loan is more anxiety-producing than a medical exam by a proctologist who uses oversized instruments.

Calculating Your Foreclosure Budget

Before you start pursuing foreclosures that you *think* you can afford, it is essential for you to *know* how much money you have available to go shopping with. Why waste valuable time and energy on properties that are too expensive, or pass up a great foreclosure purchasing opportunity because you didn't realize that it *was* in your price range after all?

The two procedures that lenders perform initially in order to "measure your financial profile" are *prequalifications* and *preapprovals*. The distinctions between the two are especially crucial when time is a critical factor and you need the money to purchase the foreclosure property quickly.

Prequalified versus Preapproved

Although many purchasers (and even people in the financial industry) use these two terms interchangeably, there is a big difference between a prequalification and a preapproval.

A *prequalification* is not much more than a lender's "over-the-phone" estimate of the interest rate, points, and so on that you will pay and the type of loan you qualify for, based on your income and your credit. *If* everything you say is true, and *if* there are no credit problems, the lender will loan you the money at the rate and terms that it quoted you. Prequalifications are conditional upon *everything*—your income, your credit history, the amount of money in your bank accounts, and so on. Nothing has been verified, and you will have to begin the process of applying for your loan from scratch after you find the foreclosure you wish to purchase and execute the sales contract with the seller.

A *preapproval*, by contrast, gives the lender a much more accurate picture of your financial status, which accelerates the time frame for obtaining a loan commitment from the lender. The same information is required as for a prequalification, including income verification, credit history, bank accounts, and so on, but, unlike what happens in a prequalification procedure, the lender processes the application forms and issues a commitment *before* you begin to look for a foreclosure. Truly authentic preapprovals are those that are signed by a lender's underwriter, with a written guarantee that the lender has issued a commitment for the loan amount and terms. The only conditions that still must be met before the lender will close are the appraisal and the title report, which *can*—in most cases—be completed within a couple of weeks. You can now focus on finding foreclosures to purchase that are within your price range, and once you sign the contract, the only things left to complete are the appraisal and the title search.

Why is this important? Preapprovals can help purchasers who are pursuing any type or all three types of foreclosure opportunities:

- When you are purchasing a foreclosure at the auction, you may be able to obtain financing from a bank within the 30-day period between the signing of the contract and the closing because, by obtaining a preapproval from the lender *before* you bid on the property, you jump-started the loan process, and it is usually realistic to assume that the appraisal and the title report can be completed by the lender in time for the closing.

- When you are purchasing an REO foreclosure after the auction, submitting a preapproval letter along with your bid or purchase offer can give you an edge over your competition if it persuades a bank or government agency that, since you are already cleared to obtain the financing and can afford to buy the property, you are a better prospect than the other bidders.

- When you are purchasing a preforeclosure, a defaulting borrower who is anxious to sell before the lender forecloses is likely to take your offer more seriously if you are already preapproved and ready to close quickly. This is also true if a lender must approve the offer you make in a short sale situation.

A Word of Caution

The downside of a preapproval is that most lenders require an inspection or appraisal, and there may be delays in getting the financing approved if, for example, the foreclosure is occupied by unfriendly people who won't allow a bank representative inside the property to inspect (or appraise) it. Also, in some cases, the lender won't approve the loan when the inspector or appraiser's report shows that the utilities are not operating and/or that extensive repairs are needed. Therefore, those who are using a preapproval to expedite the purchasing process may be limited to selecting foreclosed properties that are accessible and in good condition so that the lender's representative (i.e., the appraiser) can check the condition of the premises and the heating, electric, and plumbing systems.

Questions to Ask a Lender When Shopping for a Preapproval

When shopping for a lender that offers preapprovals, ask the following questions:

- After you are preapproved, what are the conditions that must be met in order for you to get financing? (Authentic preapprovals are already signed by an underwriter who works for a lender and has the authority to approve an applicant's loan. The preapproval is subject only to a title report and an appraisal that meets the lender's guidelines.)

- Is there a fee for the preapproval, and if so, how much is it? (Lenders usually do not charge a fee for a preapproval.)

- How long does the preapproval process take to complete? (It usually takes five to eight business days.)

- How long is the preapproval good for? (It is usually good for 60 to 90 days from commitment.)

The Burden of Proof

To clarify the terminology used in this chapter, an *applicant* is someone who is in the process of applying for a loan. The applicant becomes a *borrower* after the loan is fully executed.

The basic concept for obtaining financing is simple and straightforward. You must convince a lender to give you, the loan applicant, money to purchase a real estate property. To accomplish this, you must prove two qualifying factors. First, you must demonstrate that you have sufficient income to repay the loan. Second, in the event that you default on your promise to repay the loan and the lender forecloses, you must document, usually with a bank appraisal, that the real estate property that you pledged as security for the loan has enough value to allow the lender to recapture its losses at a foreclosure auction. The entire loan approval procedure is aimed at resolving these two issues.

Decisions, Decisions

While no one has a crystal ball to reveal what tomorrow will bring, there are some basic purchasing strategies that will help you narrow down your preferences. Once you have formulated your overall game plan, you are more likely to select a loan that is compatible with your present and future needs. Here are some important issues to consider.

How's your credit? FICO scores, developed by the Fair Isaac Corporation, are the most common credit measure used by lenders nationwide to determine a potential borrower's creditworthiness. FICO scores range from 300 (the lowest/worst score) to 850 (the highest/best score). A higher score indicates a greater likelihood that the applicant will repay his or her loan in a timely manner. Lenders use FICO scores to assess the prices and costs they will charge loan applicants. A higher score translates into a lower risk to a creditor, which is rewarded by lower interest rates and other loan fees. To calculate a person's credit score, Fair Isaac uses data collected by the three major credit bureaus: Experian, Equifax, and TransUnion. The final credit score is a compilation of data in several individual categories, including *debt, payment history, length of credit history, new credit,* and *types of credit used.* Income is not considered because lenders are not concerned only with a person's *ability* to pay; his or her *willingness* to pay is the more important factor, because people with high incomes can still be poor bill payers.

Reports vary, but only approximately 13 percent of the population has a FICO score of 800 and above; the average is approximately 723. According to the calculator on myfico.com, potential borrowers with FICO scores of 760 and up receive the best financing terms from a lender. Just as an example, if an applicant's FICO score is between 760 and 850, on a $300,000 30-year loan, he or she might pay an annual interest rate of 5.87 percent, which translates to a loan payment of $1,773 per month. By contrast, an applicant with a lower FICO score of between 580 and 619 might pay an annual interest rate of 9.25 percent, which requires a monthly loan payment of $2,469! An applicant could end up paying hundreds of thousands of dollars for the additional interest costs over the life of the loan.

Credit experts recommend the following actions for people who wish to raise their FICO scores:

1. *Pay your bills in a timely manner.* Some credit companies treat payments received only a few days late as if they were 30 days late. Therefore, payments made 30 days late on a regular basis can lower your FICO scores by 100 points.

2. *Don't close credit accounts with a long-term credit history.* A credit card with a 20-year history of timely payments is highly favored by a lending institution. Applicants who wish to downsize their credit balances are better off closing out accounts opened more recently with a shorter payment history.

3. *Minimize the number of loan applications that you file.* While it may seem prudent to apply to many lenders to see which of them can give you the best loan, each time you apply for credit, the lender requests your credit report. This request is noted as an inquiry on your credit history, and if the inquiring lender fails to provide financing after making an inquiry, it may appear that the lender found something negative in the applicant's credit history that precluded it from giving the applicant a loan, and this can have a negative effect on the applicant's FICO score. A series of inquiries made within a short time frame (e.g., two weeks) would most likely be distinguished as "comparison shopping" by FICO and would not negatively affect a FICO score, but a series of inquiries spread out over a period of months could lower your score.

4. *Minimize outstanding credit balances.* Experts recommend that consumers spend only 30 percent of their available credit limit. Credit cards that are "maxed out" to their limits can lower a person's credit score because FICO calculates the total balances in relation to available credit.

5. *"Opt out" from receiving credit cards in the mail.* A dramatic increase in cases of identity theft has proven costly to creditors. Applicants who opt out of receiving credit cards decrease the risk that arises from having too many "open" and/or "unmonitored" accounts—credit card accounts that can become vulnerable to illegal use by credit card thieves.

What type of property do you want to purchase?   The major categories of real property are residential, commercial, and industrial. These categories can be broken down further into subcategories. For example, condominiums, cooperatives, single-family homes, two-family homes, apartment buildings, and so on are subcategories of residential property. Someone who wants to purchase a single-family property will have different loan options from those available to someone who wishes to buy an office building.

Are you purchasing as an owner-occupant (who will live there) or as an investor (who will rent the property out to tenants)? An owner-occupant will usually receive a more favorable interest rate than an investor because the lender is taking less of a risk. A lender can accurately qualify an owner-occupant based on his or her individual ability to repay the loan, but an investor's ability to repay the loan is strongly influenced by the financial strength of a tenant that the investor has selected and that the lender has not qualified. In Chapter 8 we compare investor loans with loans for owner-occupants in much greater detail (also see Figure 8-1).

How long do you intend to own the property? Pinpointing your future ownership plans, that is, the length of time you wish to own the property, is an important factor in selecting the most beneficial loan for you. For example, if you intend to keep the property for more than five years, you will probably be better off with a fixed interest rate that will remain the same over the life of the loan. On the other hand, if you are buying the property with the intention of reselling it in less than five years (e.g., fixing up a handyman's special and selling it after the repairs are completed), you may be better off with a variable-rate (adjustable-rate) loan. The variable-rate loan usually begins with a lower initial rate than a fixed-rate loan, and the premises will be sold before periodic increases elevate the interest rate higher than a fixed rate would have been.

How many years do you want the loan to last before it is paid off? The length of the loan term (15 years, 30 years, or some other term) usually influences the loan's interest rate, the monthly loan payment, and the borrower's equity. In comparing a 15-year loan with a 30-year loan, generally a 15-year loan has a quicker equity buildup and a lower interest rate, but the monthly payment is higher than it would be for a 30-year loan. The differences between 15- and 30-year loans are discussed in more detail later in this chapter.

Will you apply for a conventional loan or a government-backed loan? In return for deep discounts on interest rates and other loan costs, government-backed loans may have more restrictive qualifying criteria than conventional loans. Government loans may also have guidelines that regulate the minimum and maximum purchase price of the property, the amount of the down payment, the amount of family income, the length of time the borrower pledges to occupy the property, whether or not the applicant is required to be a first-time buyer, and other such factors. Government-backed loans are discussed in more detail later in this chapter.

Are you interested in buying a "handyman's special" or a property that is already in "move-in condition"? Some lenders require verification that the plumbing, heating, and electrical systems are operable before approving the loans. Someone who is purchasing a handyman's special that requires extensive renovation work could face lengthy delays in obtaining financing under those circumstances and should apply for a loan with a lender that does not "condition" its loan approval on the "condition" of the property.

Types of Loans

The following section will help applicants understand the different types of loans that are available.

Conventional Fixed-Rate Loans

The first type of loan is a conventional fixed-rate loan with monthly interest payments that do not fluctuate over the life of the loan. Conventional 30-year loans offer absolute certainty on housing costs (aside from annual increases in property taxes and/or homeowner's insurance premiums if the lender maintains an escrow account and collects monthly payments from the borrower to distribute to the tax collection authority and the insurance company). Conventional 15-year loans have lower interest rates than 30-year loans because the quicker payoff allows a lender to put the money to work again sooner by lending it to a new borrower.

Figure 6-1 illustrates the outcome when the same amount of money is borrowed for a 15-year term and for a 30-year term. Utilizing the free loan amortization calculator provided by bankrate.com, Borrower A's $300,000 loan is amortized over 30 years at a 7 percent interest rate, and the monthly principal and interest payment is $1,995.91. Borrower B's $300,000 loan, amortized over 15 years, has a reduced interest rate (anywhere from one-quarter to one-half of a percent lower). At 6½ percent interest, the monthly principal and interest payment is $2,613.32, or $617.41 per month more than Borrower A's monthly payment. Borrower B's higher monthly payment requires more provable income

A 15-YEAR LOAN VERSUS A 30-YEAR LOAN*

Borrower A's 30-year loan after 5 years

Original loan amount	$300,000
Interest rate paid	7%
Monthly payment (principal + interest)	$1,995.91
Total amount paid over 5 years	$119,754
Total interest paid over 5 years	$102,149
Total principal paid over 5 years	$17,605
Loan balance after 5 years	$282,395

Borrower B's 15-year loan after 5 years*

Original loan amount	$300,000
Interest rate paid	6.50%
Monthly payment (principal + interest)	$2,613.32
Total amount paid over 5 years	$156,799
Total interest paid over 5 years	$86,951
Total principal paid over 5 years	$69,848
Loan balance after 5 years	$230,152

*Rounded to the nearest dollar.

Figure 6-1. A comparison between a 15-year and a 30-year loan after 5 years.

than Borrower A must show, but Borrower B's 15-year loan offers faster equity buildup and a quicker payoff than Borrower A's 30-year loan. If you were to freeze the loan accounts of Borrower A and Borrower B after five years, the differences in the status of the two loans are quite significant.

Borrower B's monthly payment is only $617.41 more per month than Borrower A's payment, yet, after five years, Borrower B has paid off $69,848.52 on the 15-year loan compared to $17,605.38 paid off by Borrower A on the 30-year loan.

The equity buildup and quicker payoff features are obvious benefits for applicants who choose the 15-year loan, but many people are reluctant to commit to the higher monthly payments. In this case those who choose the 30-year loan because of the lower monthly payments can still reduce the term of the loan by making extra payments during the year without committing to the higher monthly payment required for the 15-year loan. (When making extra payments, you should include clear instructions for the lender to apply the additional amounts to the principal of the loan, as opposed to applying the extra amount to the escrow account that may have been set up by the lender for property taxes and/or property insurance.) With a conventional loan, the additional amounts paid by the borrower do not reduce the monthly payments. Instead, the principal of the loan will be paid off sooner, reducing the number of years before the loan is paid in full.

The benefit of a conventional loan is derived from the security of fixed monthly payments that it provides. The downside is that the applicant usually needs a fairly unblemished credit report in order to receive the most favorable interest rate, lowest closing costs, and so on.

Adjustable-Rate Loans

Adjustable-rate (or variable-rate) loans are loans where the interest rate changes in accordance with a prearranged schedule. The most common payment schedules are six-month, one-year, three-year, or five-year terms. On each anniversary date of the loan, the payments are adjusted based on the prevailing rate of interest.

The benefit of this type of loan is that it generally offers lower initial rates than a fixed-rate loan, and it may be assumable by new buyers. Adjustable-rate loans also offer the possibility of future rate decreases, and may even be convertible to fixed-rate programs after a period of time that is contractually agreed to as part of the loan terms. The downside is that this type of loan carries the risk of interest-rate increases, which means that monthly payments could increase significantly in future years if interest rates were to skyrocket.

FHA/DVA Loans

Federal Housing Administration (FHA) and Department of Veterans Affairs (DVA) loans are backed by the federal government. The benefits include lower down-payment requirements, and in some cases, especially for first-time buyers with good credit, the loans may be assumable with no prepayment penalty. The downside is that these types of loans may require higher closing costs than conventional loans, and there may be application red tape and delays in obtaining loan approvals.

Balloon Loans

Balloon loans are most commonly found in situations where the seller holds the loan (or holds paper), which means that the borrower (who is also the buyer in this case) makes payments to the seller each month instead of to a bank.

Balloon loans may offer the borrower lower rates and other flexible terms, especially when the loan is provided by the seller, but at the end of the loan term, the entire remaining balance is still due in a "balloon," or lump-sum, payment requiring the borrower to obtain new financing to pay off the loan.

This type of arrangement is advantageous to a borrower who is unable to obtain bank financing because of insufficient provable income (e.g., a borrower who owns a cash business), or who has minor problems with her credit rating, not enough time at her current job, or a past bankruptcy. The borrower benefits by avoiding expensive closing costs, such as points and origination fees, that a lending institution would have charged if this was a traditional loan. Sellers benefit by attracting a wider range of buyers who don't want to wait several more years for their credit to improve in order to own their own homes. At the end of the loan term (most commonly between one and five years), when the balloon payment for the remaining principal balance becomes due, the borrower should be in a better position to obtain financing from another source, usually a lending institution. By this time the borrower has had a chance to show sufficient provable income on his or her tax return to qualify for a new loan or to clear up the credit problems that previously prevented him or her from qualifying for a loan. The borrower obtains the new financing, pays off the balance of the purchase price to the seller, and makes future monthly loan payments to the new lender. On the negative side, this type of loan could be disadvantageous if housing prices decline before the balloon becomes due, and, since the property is worth less, the balloon loan exceeds the property's value and the buyer cannot obtain enough financing to pay off the balloon loan balance.

Interest-Only Loans

Some loans require interest-only payments, with the borrower's payments covering only the interest that is due and providing no reduction in the principal of the loan. The interest is usually paid by the borrower on a monthly basis.

The advantage to the borrower is that since he or she is paying only the loan interest each month, the monthly payment is lower than it would be for a borrower whose payment was reducing the principal of the loan as well as paying the interest. The downside of an interest-only loan is that it builds no equity; at the end of the loan term, the borrower still owes the full amount of the principal. This can be of particular concern when real estate properties decline in value; since the borrower still owes the full loan balance, the amount of the loan may exceed the property's value.

Graduated-Payment Loans

Graduated-payment loans are loans in which the payment increases by preset amounts during the first few years and then stabilizes at a fixed interest rate. The difference between this type of loan and an adjustable-rate loan is that with a graduated-payment loan, you know in advance the percentage by which the interest rate will increase for the term of the loan instead of relying on changeable market rates, as you do with an adjustable-rate loan.

The benefit of this type of loan is that it allows a borrower to begin paying the loan at a lower interest rate that he or she can afford now, with the understanding that the rates will increase gradually. Borrowers who select this type of loan presume that the periodic increases in the interest rates will be offset by an elevated salary level as the borrower's job-related experience leads to a higher earning capacity. The downside is that the borrower's earning capacity may not increase as rapidly as anticipated, or that even if his or her earnings increase, unexpected expenses (e.g., a baby) could cancel out (or exceed) the additional income that was earmarked to offset the higher loan payment.

Home Equity Loans

A *home equity loan* (a.k.a. HEL) is a loan that allows you to tap into the equity in your home to help finance a down payment on another home, major home repairs, medical bills, or a college education.

Home equity loans are most commonly second-position liens (second trust deeds). Home equity loans come in two types, *closed end* and *open end*. Both types are usually referred to as second or junior liens or second trust deeds. Home equity loans and lines of credit are usually, but not always, for a shorter term than first liens. Depending on your financial situation and what you used the loan for, the Internal Revenue Service may allow you to deduct home equity loan interest from your income taxes. (Check with your accountant for more information.)

Closed-end home equity loans   When you obtain a *closed-end home equity loan (HEL),* you receive a lump sum at the closing, and you cannot borrow further amounts. The maximum amount of money that you can borrow is determined by such factors as your credit history, your income, and the appraised value of the property you are borrowing against. State banking laws govern the percentage of equity that a lender may allow you to borrow. Some lenders may allow financing of up to 100 percent of the appraised value of the home minus any existing financing; others may allow borrowing of only up to 80 percent of equity. Closed-end home equity loans generally have fixed rates and can be repaid over periods usually up to 15 years. Some home equity loans offer a reduced payoff term, whereby at the end of the term, the remaining balance is due in a lump sum (a balloon payment). These lump-sum payments can be avoided by paying more than the minimum monthly amount due and applying the additional payment toward the principal balance or by refinancing the loan and paying off the balloon.

Open-end home equity loan   Also known as an *open-end revolving credit line* or a *home equity line of credit (HELOC),* this type of loan allows you a maximum draw rather than requiring you to borrow a fixed dollar amount. Unlike the closed-end HEL, which requires the amount borrowed to be paid to you in full at the closing, the open-end HELOC allows the lender to advance you *up to* the amount you need when you want to borrow it, based on criteria similar to those for closed-end loans.

Like the closed-end HEL, HELOCs may allow you to borrow up to100 percent of the value of a home, less any existing financing; however, HELOC lines of credit can be repaid at terms up to 30 years, at fixed or adjustable interest rates.

Like HELs, most HELOCs are secured by second or junior liens or trust deeds. An increasing number, however, are first liens; for example, you could use the line of credit to refinance your existing home loan. Once the HELOC line of credit is approved, you can draw on it by writing a check, using a special credit card, or some other such method.

HELOCs have a *draw period,* during which time you can use the line of credit, and a *repayment period,* during which the money you borrowed must be repaid. During the draw period, usually 5 to 10 years, you are required to pay only interest on the amount you borrowed.

During the repayment period, usually 10 to 20 years, you must repay the loan. Some HELOCs, however, require you to repay the entire balance at the end of the draw period in a balloon payment, in which case you would have to refinance.

The annual percentage rate (APR) on a traditional loan reflects points and other up-front loan costs; the APR on a HELOC is based on the interest rate alone. Up-front costs are relatively low. On a $150,000 HELOC, loan costs seldom exceed $1,000, and in many cases they are paid by the lender without a rate increase.

While most HELOCs are repaid with an adjustable interest loan, some HELOCs are convertible into fixed-rate loans at the time the funds are drawn. This is a useful option for borrowers who draw a large amount at one time and want the security of a fixed interest rate during the repayment period.

The major disadvantage of a HELOC without a fixed interest rate option is its exposure to interest-rate hikes. If the prime rate changes on April 30, the HELOC rate will change effective May 1. Another exception is HELOCs with a guaranteed introductory rate, but these rates are usually in effect for only a few months and revert to an adjustable interest rate loan thereafter.

Piggyback Loans

A *piggyback loan* is a home financing option that allows a buyer to purchase a property with loans from one or more lenders.

There are three popular varieties of piggyback loans: the *80-10-10 loan*, the *80-20 loan* (also known as the 80-20-0 loan), and the *80-15-5 loan*. The first number indicates that 80 percent of the home's purchase price will be financed by a loan from the first lender; the second number indicates the percentage amount of a loan secured by a second loan from a different lender (which could be a HELOC); and the third number indicates the down payment percentage. For example, if you select the 80-10-10 loan, 80 percent of the home's purchase price will be financed by the first lender, 10 percent of the purchase price will be financed by the second lender, and you will pay 10 percent of the purchase price in cash as the down payment. If you select the 80-20 loan, 80 percent of the purchase price will be financed by the first lender, 20 percent of the loan will be financed by the second lender, and your down payment will be $0.

The benefit of a piggyback loan is that it helps more people qualify for a home. A borrower with little or no down payment should have better luck with the loan approval process on a piggyback loan than on a single conventional loan because more than one lender is involved in the loan transaction, which spreads the entire loan risk between multiple lenders.

On the downside, the combined rates for piggyback loans are often higher than those for standard loans. Although the lender who is financing only 80 percent of the loan amount might be willing to drop its rates a bit, the second lender, who is financing only 5 to 20 percent of the loan, won't benefit from lending the money unless it can realize a high interest rate on its money. In addition, piggyback loans may require a large balloon payment at the end of the loan term. This can be a big problem for borrowers who fail to plan ahead by setting aside extra money every month in order to pay the balloon. Another disadvantage occurs if property values fall. If the loan exceeds the property value, the borrower may not be able to obtain enough financing to pay off the balance of the balloon loan. One final disadvantage is that the dual loans may have eaten up all of the equity in the property; therefore, if an emergency were to arise that affected the borrower's income, it is unlikely that the borrower would be able to cash out his or her equity in the house with an additional mortgage or home equity loan to help pay his or her living expenses during the emergency period.

Comparison Shopping for the Best Lender

There are two very important reasons for putting your time and effort into shopping for the loan that is right for you. First, you avoid wasting your time and money applying for a loan that does not suit your financial situation. Second, you avoid loans with inflated interest rates and other overpriced costs.

Begin by organizing your questions and answers onto a spreadsheet so that you can compare prices. To accomplish this, the method that I

Name of Lending Institution	Question #1	Question #2	Question #3	Question #4	Question #5	Question #6	Question #7	Question #8	etc.
ABC Bank									
DEF Bank									
XYZ Bank									
etc.									

Figure 6-2. A sample spreadsheet for comparing mortgage programs offered by lending institutions.

devised for myself (and still find to be the most effective way to comparison shop) can be completed in three steps.

Step 1: List the names of the lending institutions that you wish to contact on the left side of the spreadsheet.

Step 2: Arrange the questions that you want to ask each lender across the top of the spreadsheet. (See Figure 6-2.)

Step 3: Call each of the lenders on your list, ask the questions from Step 2, and fill in the answers on your spreadsheet. When you are finished, you will have an organized overview of the loan packages available, allowing you to compare each lender with its competitors and select the lender that offers the best loan for you.

Key Questions to Ask a Lender

For Fixed- and Adjustable-Rate Loans, Ask the Following Questions

How long must applicants have been employed at their present jobs to qualify for a loan? Some lending institutions require loan applicants to have been working at their present jobs for a certain length of time (commonly two years). Some lenders are more flexible and will take specific circumstances into consideration, such as a job transfer. What the lender does not want to see is a history of job-hopping or other inconsistent patterns of short-term employment that can interrupt the steady flow of income that the applicant needs in order to pay the loan in the future.

Does the lender follow FNMA guidelines or hold the loans in its own portfolio? When banks lend money to borrowers, the borrowers sign a note (promising to repay the loan) and a mortgage or deed of trust (pledging the property as collateral, or security, for the loan). The security instrument may be sold in the secondary market if it meets the requisite guidelines, after which the bank "recycles" the money received from the sale of the instrument into new loans for the next applicants. The Federal National Mortgage Association—Fannie Mae—(introduced in Chapter 4 as a potential source of foreclosure listings) is the largest purchaser of residential real estate loans in the secondary market. In order for lending institutions to sell loans to Fannie Mae, the loans must "conform to" certain conditions that are clearly enumerated in "Fannie Mae Guidelines." There is a maximum loan amount that can be sold to Fannie Mae, and this maximum amount increases periodically. Loans that exceed the Fannie Mae limit are called "jumbo" loans.

If a loan cannot be sold to Fannie Mae, the lender keeps the loan in its own portfolio. The lender's qualifying criteria for loans that it intends to keep in its portfolio may be more lenient or more stringent than Fannie Mae's qualifying criteria. For example, one lender may require applicants to have a blemish-free credit rating for loans that it keeps in its portfolio; another lender may be more concerned with the applicant's income-to-debt ratio (income minus expenses); and still another may prefer an applicant to have a higher loan-to-value ratio (more equity in the property). Knowledge of lenders' guidelines can be extremely valuable to foreclosure purchasers who are willing to put effort into finding the right lender. For instance, applicants can capitalize on their pristine credit by applying to a lender that rewards perfect credit ratings by offering much lower interest rates than its competitors are offering.

Can the interest rate on the loan be locked in?   If you want to ensure that the interest rate you are quoted remains the same until the closing, you can ask for the rate to be locked in. Ask the lender how much it would cost for the lock-in and find out what would happen if interest rates go down. Would you get the benefit of the lower rate? If not, the lock-in option may not be favorable because you could be penalized by being locked into a higher rate than you could have had without the lock-in.

What is the prevailing interest rate?   The prevailing rate is the interest rate the lender is charging for the loan at the time of the quote. The prevailing rate can change daily.

How many points are being charged?   A point is another name for pre-paid interest and equals 1 percent of the loan (not the purchase price) that the applicant is applying for. For example, on a $300,000 loan, one point equals $3,000.

Is there an origination fee, and if so, how much is it?   An origination fee is an administrative expense that many lenders charge as part of the loan cost. Lenders do not always charge an origination fee, nor are they required to do so. If the lender does charge an origination fee, the amount can range from $100 to several points.

How much is the application fee?   The application fee is the amount that a lender charges the applicant to "open the file" when it begins the application process. The application fee usually includes charges for a credit report and an appraisal of the property. There may be other fees as well. If the lender charges an application fee, ask if any part of the fee is refundable if the loan application is denied, or if the applicant does not accept the loan terms that the lender offers.

Is the loan assumable?   Assumable loans are loans that can be taken over by a purchaser who wishes to leave the existing loan intact. The purchaser pays the difference between the asking price and the loan balance in cash, and assumes the loan balance, along with the responsibility for making future monthly payments to the lender. With an assumable loan, the purchaser may not have to qualify for a new loan from scratch, which in turn expedites the property transfer.

If the loan is assumable, find out what the procedure for someone to assume it involves. In some cases, the person who assumes the loan must be requalified by the lender (i.e., the loan is assumable with bank permission). In other cases, the lending institution will permit the purchaser to assume the loan by signing some papers and sometimes paying a nominal administrative fee.

Is there a prepayment penalty? A prepayment penalty is an extra charge to a borrower who pays off the loan balance before the end of the loan term, usually either by refinancing or by selling the property and paying off the loan in full. Federal laws may limit the amount that banks can charge for prepayment penalties.

Does the lender escrow for property taxes and property insurance? Many lenders require borrowers to provide a reserve or escrow fund to accrue money for future real estate taxes and/or homeowner's insurance premiums. When the loan is made, the lender opens a reserve account on behalf of the borrower. The monthly loan payment includes the payment toward the Principal of the loan, Interest on the loan, Taxes, and Insurance, also known as the monthly PITI. The lender accumulates the payments toward taxes and insurance in an escrow account, or reserve fund, and when the taxes or insurance premiums are due, the lender forwards the taxes to the tax collector and the insurance premiums to the insurance company. By controlling the monthly collection of the payments from the borrowers and their timely remittance to the creditors, the lender can protect its interests in the property. You will need to know how many months of escrow the lender will collect at the closing. Depending on the state in which the property is located, the property tax and insurance escrows can be one of the more expensive closing costs. Federal laws limit the number of months of escrow reserves that lenders can require borrowers to pay in advance.

How many months of assets (i.e., cash) does the lender require applicants to have available in their bank accounts for the loan to close? Some lenders require applicants to have enough money available in savings after the closing to cover one or two months of loan payments (including property taxes and property insurance if the bank is escrowing for those expenses) in the event that an emergency interrupts the applicant's income.

Does the lender require "seasoning" before approving a loan? Some lenders require an applicant who wishes to obtain a loan on a home that he or she already owns and now wishes to obtain financing on to own that home for one or two years (a.k.a. "a seasoned ownership") before applying for a new loan.

Will the lender consider the credit limits on the applicant's credit cards as debt? As discussed earlier in this chapter in the discussion of FICO scores, when calculating the applicant's income-to-debt ratio, lenders look at the credit lines on the applicant's credit cards. Even though the applicant pays the balance in full each month and has no outstanding balance due, some lenders take into account the possibility that the applicant could, at any time, go out and borrow up to the limit on all of his or her credit cards. If it is the lender's policy to consider the applicant's maximum limits as debt even when there is no outstanding balance, someone who is in this situation and applies for a loan with that lender may be wasting his or her time and/or money for the application fee. In some cases, the situation can easily be remedied by having the applicant close out the credit card accounts and/or lower the limits on the lines of credit before applying for a loan. Another alternative is for the applicant to select a lender that considers only the outstanding credit card balances (and not the credit limit) in calculating the income-to-debt ratios.

For Adjustable-Rate Loans Only, Ask the Following Questions

What index does the lender use? The index is the bank's rate of borrowing, or the amount that the lender is charged to put money out on the street to borrowers. All lenders use one specific index, which is specified within the loan documents. The current rate of that index can be found in most local newspapers. Interest rates on adjustable-rate loans are recalculated according to the average of the index.

What is the lender's margin? The lender's margin is the percentage of profit the bank wants to make above the index. This amount remains the same over the term of the loan. It is calculated as follows:

$$\boxed{\text{Index} + \text{Margin} = \text{Prevailing Rate of Interest}}$$

If the rate of borrowing (index) is 7 percent and the margin (profit) is 2 percent, then the rate that is quoted is 9 percent.

How often are the rates adjusted? The most common adjustment periods are six months, one year, and three years. This means that interest rates, and, as a result, the monthly loan payment, will be adjusted on the loan's six-month, one-year, or three-year anniversary.

What is the term cap?   The term cap is the maximum amount that the interest rate can go up or down during each adjustment period.

What is the life cap?   The life cap is the maximum amount that the interest rate can go up or down during the life of the loan. For example, on a 30-year loan with a life cap of 16 percent, the interest rate may fluctuate up to or below that amount, but may never exceed it.

What year does the lender use as a basis for qualifying an applicant? When calculating an applicant's qualifying ratios for an adjustable-rate loan, lenders frequently do so using the maximum anticipated increase (up to the term cap) on the loan's first anniversary.

Thus, an applicant who applies for a one-year adjustable loan with a 2 percent term cap, and is locked in at a 7 percent interest rate for the first year, will most likely be qualified based on the maximum rate the loan could adjust to on its first anniversary: a 7 percent initial rate + a 2 percent maximum term cap = 9 percent.

Is the adjustable-rate loan convertible to a fixed-rate loan, and if so, what is the procedure?   Adjustable-rate loans with a convertible feature are popular because borrowers can start off paying the lower initial interest rate on the adjustable loan, while retaining the option of converting to a fixed-rate loan later on. The procedures to follow and the costs involved with the fixed-rate conversion are set forth in the loan documents. Some lenders allow the borrower to convert the loan to a fixed rate after the first year by paying a small administrative fee, while other lenders require the applicant to wait for several years before the conversion feature becomes available.

Is the loan negatively amortized?   Normally, homeowners expect to reduce the principal balance of the amount they borrowed when they make their monthly loan payments. However, when the prevailing rate (index + margin) exceeds the maximum term cap allowed, the extra cost is passed along to the borrower if the loan is negatively amortized, and the loan balance can increase instead of growing smaller as time goes on.

As an example, assume that we have a loan with a 7 percent interest rate and a 1 percent term cap. For the period prior to its 1-year anniversary, the index on the loan averaged a 2 percent interest rate increase. The new interest rate should be 9 percent, but because of the 1 percent term cap, the maximum interest-rate increase is to 8 percent.

In an amortized loan, the lender would absorb the 1 percent difference between the 9 percent that the borrower should have been paying and the 8 percent that he is capped at. In a negatively amortized loan, however, the lender can require the borrower to remit payment for the negative difference before the new loan period begins, or the lender will add the amount to the borrower's loan balance. If the amount is added to the loan balance, when the new monthly payments are calculated, the lender will base the borrower's payments on the increased loan balance.

In this chapter, we covered the most popular forms of traditional financing that are available for foreclosure purchasers. Those who wish to pursue more creative approaches to financing foreclosures will find them in Chapter 7.

7

Creative Strategies for Financing Foreclosures

Whether you have a lot of cash, very little cash, good credit, or tarnished credit, there are a number of creative strategies that can be implemented in conjunction with, or as a replacement for, traditional loan financing. Chapter 7 provides examples of these initiatives for each of the four categories of foreclosure purchasers:

Category 1: Foreclosure purchasers with limited cash and good credit
Category 2: Foreclosure purchasers with limited cash and tarnished credit
Category 3: Foreclosure purchasers with a lot of cash and good credit
Category 4: Foreclosure purchasers with a lot of cash and tarnished credit

Please note that the numbers in Chapter 7 are for demonstration purposes only. In some parts of the country, housing prices for residential properties and housing costs, including property taxes and homeowner's insurance, are lower than the numbers set forth in this chapter; and in some parts of the country, the prices will be higher.

Category 1: Foreclosure Purchasers with Limited Cash and Good Credit

People in Category 1 who wish to purchase foreclosures should consider the following creative financing strategies.

Put the Equity in Your Home to Good Use

If you currently own a home and you have lived there for a number of years, the equity* you have accumulated can be a valuable resource to tap for financing another property. Let's say that 10 years ago, you purchased a handyman's special for $200,000, paid $20,000 as a down payment, and took out a loan to finance the remaining $180,000 Depending on how much the property values in your area have appreciated, and especially if you have made improvements to the premises, the value of your home may have increased substantially during the time you've owned it.

If the house is your primary dwelling, you can refinance the existing loan or, if you have already paid off the loan, you can apply for a new one. (An investment property may be more difficult to refinance.)

* The equity in your home is calculated by subtracting the remaining loan balance from the current market value.

Another option is to apply for a junior lien in the form of an equity loan and/or an equity line of credit (see the discussion of HELs and HELOCs in Chapter 6) and use the proceeds to purchase your foreclosure. The difference in obtaining an equity loan option is that the loan-to-value ratio may be limited to 70 percent ($210,000) whereas the refinance option may allow up to 80 percent ($240,000). Figure 7-1 illustrates the refinancing option, and Figure 7-2 illustrates the junior lien option.

The benefit of tapping into the equity in your present home is that you keep the property you have and use the equity in that property to buy more real estate, which will also appreciate over time. Whether you are an investor who plans to rent out the foreclosure you purchase to a tenant, whose monthly rent payment covers all or most of the monthly amount of your new loan, or you plan to fix it up and sell it for a profit, you have used your money to buy another appreciable asset and, consequently, to increase your wealth.

REFINANCING A 10-YEAR-OLD LOAN WITH A NEW LOAN

Initial purchase price 10 years ago	$200,000
Down payment	$20,000
Initial loan balance 10 years ago	$180,000 (30 years @ 7%)
Current property value	$300,000
Refinance amount available	$240,000 (80% of current property value)
Less: Remaining loan balance (if repaid monthly without extra payments to reduce the loan balance)	$154,000 (approximately)
Cash available for refinance	$86,000 (approximately)

Note: To calculate the amount of cash available, deduct the remaining loan balance (approximately $154,000) from the refinance amount available of $240,000. Some lenders may also deduct closing costs for the refinancing, which will reduce the amount of cash available.

Figure 7-1. Refinancing a 10-year-old loan with a new loan.

TAKING OUT AN EQUITY LOAN/LINE OF CREDIT AS A JUNIOR LIEN

Initial purchase price 10 years ago	$200,000
Down payment	$20,000
Initial loan balance 10 years ago	$180,000 (30 years @ 7%)
Current property value	$300,000
Refinance amount	$210,000 (70% of current property value)
Less: Remaining loan balance (if repaid monthly without extra payments to reduce the loan balance)	$154,000 (approximately)
Cash available for junior lien	$56,000 (approximately)

Note: To calculate the amount of cash available, deduct the remaining loan balance (approximately $154,000) from the refinance amount available of $210,000. Some lenders may also deduct closing costs for the junior lien, which will reduce the amount of cash available.

Figure 7-2. Taking out an equity loan/line of credit as a junior lien.

Obtain Financing from Banks and Government Agencies to Purchase (REO) Foreclosures from Their Inventories

If you have decided to buy a bank-owned foreclosure from a lending institution's inventory (a.k.a. an REO), or a government-owned fore-closure from HUD, the DVA, the FDIC, the GSA, and so on, the bank or government agency generally has the authority and the motivation to offer extremely favorable financing terms on loans it provides for people who purchase properties in its inventories. As I mentioned in Chapters 3 and 4, lending institutions and government agencies are *not* in the business of managing and selling real estate and would much rather provide financing so that people can buy the properties instead of keeping them in their inventories and paying for costly maintenance charges. The benefits of obtaining financing from banks and government agencies include discounts on interest rates and closing costs, lower down payment requirements, and so on.

Obtain Financing from a Foreclosing Lender before a Property Is Auctioned

In some cases, when a loan is in default, the foreclosing lender will agree to allow a purchaser to assume the loan balance before the property goes to auction (see Chapter 5). The foreclosing lender may even agree to waive some of the late charges and back payments that have recently accrued. When a loan is in default, it is clearly more advantageous for the lender to substitute a new borrower who is financially capable of paying the monthly payments and who is willing to assume the delinquent borrower's loan balance. The benefit to the purchaser is the possibility of homeownership by assuming the loan balance—even with new repayment terms that are different from those the lender has with the defaulting borrower—with little or no cash outlay. The downside for the new purchaser is the expense of applying for a new loan if the foreclosing lender requires the new purchaser to obtain financing instead of allowing the existing loan to be assumed.

Get Your Foot in the Door with a Hard-Money Loan

Another option for financing a foreclosure is a hard-money loan. This is not "break-your-arm" financing from a loan shark. It is a financing tool that is driven by the equity in the property, rather than by the borrower's good credit rating. The benefit of this type of loan is its availability to applicants within a few days. It is, therefore, very desirable when fast cash is needed. The drawbacks are the high points and high interest rates charged. Consequently, this form of financing is recommended only for a short period of time. You should replace it with a new loan bearing a lower interest rate as soon as possible.

Build Wealth through Contract Transfers

Another way that people can build up enough money to purchase a foreclosure is through profits on contract transfers. In many cases, the sales contract issued to the high bidder at the auction is assignable (transferable), unless there is language in the contract that expressly forbids assignment. Since the successful bidder is expected to come up with cash for the purchase, the sale is not contingent upon the buyer's ability to secure financing. Therefore, the contract can be transferred to a new buyer, as long as the new buyer has the money required to close. Also known as "flipping the contract," people have made a lucrative business out of successfully bidding on properties at auctions and then assigning the contracts to other buyers before the closing. The new buyer refunds the original bidder's down payment plus an agreed-upon profit, and becomes the new contract vendee.

As illustrated in Figure 7-3, let's assume that you are bidding on a property that is worth $325,000. You purchase it at the auction for $275,000. You give the referee, sheriff, or trustee $27,500 as the 10 percent down payment. There is $247,500 due at closing. You assign the contract to a new buyer, and the new buyer pays you a down payment of $42,500, which is a reimbursement of your $27,500 down payment plus a (totally negotiable) profit of $15,000. The new buyer closes with $247,500 still due to the seller from your original contract. The benefit to the new buyer is purchasing a $325,000 property for $290,000. You earned a quick $15,000 for bidding and assigning the contract to someone else.

It is important to remember that this technique generally works only for cash purchases. When there is financing from the foreclosing

---

CONTRACT TRANSFERS

Property value: $325,000

Purchase price: $275,000

Original Bidder (You)	New Buyer
$275,000 purchase price	$290,000 purchase price
$27,500 down payment	$42,500 down payment
$247,500 due at closing	$247,500 due at closing

Benefits to new buyer: $325,000 property for $290,000

Benefits to original bidder (you): $15,000 profit (for assigning contract)

Figure 7-3. A contract transfer.

lender involved (i.e., when you purchase an REO and the bank or government agency that owns the property agrees to give you financing), then the loan will be contingent upon your credit history and income and usually will not be assignable. Before you attempt this strategy, research the terms of the sale carefully to ascertain whether the contract will allow assignment.

The downside risk in contract transfer arrangements can be significant. You must be certain that the new buyer to whom you assigned your contract is financially able to come up with the cash for the closing. If the new buyer is not able to close, you may still be contractually required to complete the transaction as the original contract vendee, and if you are unable to do so, you risk forfeiting your down payment. Additional penalties may be also be imposed pursuant to the terms of sale (as discussed in Chapter 2 in the section "No Down Payment Refunds").

Borrow against Whole Life Insurance Policies (Are You Sitting on Hidden Treasure?)

Have you owned a whole life insurance policy for a number of years? If so, then chances are you've accumulated a good amount of cash in that policy by now, and you may have some options to consider.

You can use the cash in your policy to buy a foreclosure. Or you can borrow money from a bank using the cash in your policy as collateral and assign the ownership of the policy to the bank. Finally, you can take out a loan from a bank based on the policy's cash value. Using the cash you have accumulated in your policy as collateral, you can repay the loan and pay a fraction of the interest rate you would have paid on a typical personal or property loan. Contact your insurance agent to discuss the viability of this financing alternative in your particular circumstances.

Category 2: Foreclosure Purchasers with Limited Cash and Tarnished Credit

People in Category 2 who wish to purchase foreclosures should consider these alternatives.

Buy Foreclosures with Partners

It has become increasingly popular for people to purchase foreclosures with partners. There are many wealthy professionals out there with great credit ratings and lots of cash, but with no time to do the legwork that plays an essential role in any foreclosure purchase. If your funds are limited, but you have the time and the knowledge to acquire foreclosures, then you can offer those services as your contribution to the partnership.

People in Category 2 need to build up their credit and their finances, which can be a slow process. For those of you without enough cash to go out and buy a foreclosure, partnerships are an ideal way to help you accomplish your goals even when you are not yet able to do so independently. With each new venture, the profits that you earn will continue to accumulate, until eventually you will find yourself in a position where you have enough money to purchase a foreclosure without partners.

There are many benefits to all parties that can be derived from this type of arrangement, including the pooling of expertise and financial backing, the ability to share expenses, and, if you are new at this endeavor, the security of having the support of partners who share the same interests as you. The downside is that this type of partnership usually involves a sharing of control, which could lead to many disagreements unless each partner's role is clearly defined in a written agreement.

An overview of partnership functions and roles. Partnerships formed for the purpose of purchasing foreclosures may be organized in several ways.

The "cash" contributor's function is to provide the money with which the partnership will purchase (and repair) the property.

The "time and legwork" contributor's function is to locate a foreclosure and provide documented evidence for the other partner(s) that the property is a good investment. These preliminary preparations are covered in greater detail in Chapter 9. Other duties for the time and legwork partner might include providing an analysis of the property's current market value prior to repairs, calculating the anticipated purchase price, obtaining estimates for the costs and time to complete the repairs (see Chapter 13 for more details about hiring a contractor), and estimating the anticipated sales price after the repairs are completed.

Variations of partnerships. Figures 7-4 and 7-5 illustrate two completely different partnership arrangements: one with four people (an organizer plus three cash contributors) and one with three people (three equal partners). The partnership with four people (Figure 7-4) is formed when one of the partners will be contributing time, legwork and knowledge and the three other partners will be contributing cash. The partnership with three equal partners (Figure 7-5) is formed when all three partners are equal cash contributors.

An organizer plus three equal partners. Figure 7-4 illustrates a variation where four people purchase as partners. One partner (Partner 1) generally has the least (if any) cash to purchase a foreclosure, but instead contributes his expertise and time to find the best foreclosure in accordance

BUYING WITH PARTNERS: ORGANIZER PLUS THREE CASH CONTRIBUTORS

☐ The Roles of Four Partners

Partner 1

Role	Organizer
Contribution	Expertise, legwork, no cash investment

Partners 2, 3, and 4

Role	Financial
Contribution	$60,000 cash each
Breakdown	$50,000 each toward purchase price
	$10,000 each toward repair costs
Total cash outlay	$180,000

☐ Foreclosure Purchase—Cost Analysis

Purchase price	$150,000
Add: repairs cost	$30,000
Total costs	$180,000

The four partners sell the property after all necessary repairs have been made.

☐ Foreclosure Sale—Profit Analysis

Sales price	$300,000
Each partner's split	$75,000 each (4 equal shares)
Partner 1	**$75,000 profit**
Partners 2, 3, and 4	**$15,000 profit ($75,000 − $60,000 investment)**
	25% return on investment

Figure 7-4. A sample partnership arrangement: organizer plus three partners.

BUYING WITH PARTNERS: THREE EQUAL CASH CONTRIBUTORS

☐ Partners 1, 2, and 3

Role	Financial
Contribution	$60,000 cash each ($50,000 purchase + $10,000 repairs)
Total cash outlay	$180,000

☐ Foreclosure Purchase—Cost Analysis

Purchase price	$150,000
Repairs	$30,000
Total cost	$180,000

☐ Foreclosure Sale—Profit Analysis

Sales price	$300,000
Each partner's split	$100,000 each (3 equal shares)
Partners 1, 2, and 3	**$40,000 profit (66.6% return on investment)**

Figure 7-5. A sample partnership arrangement: three equal partners.

with the goals set forth in the partnership agreement. In this case, Partner 1 has no cash investment but is the person who locates, inspects and performs all of the legwork necessary to procure the property for the partnership. Partners 2, 3, and 4 each contribute $50,000 cash to purchase the property for $150,000 plus another $10,000 each toward repairs, for a total contribution of $60,000. In our example, after the contractual period elapses, the partners sell the house for $300,000. If the $300,000 is split four ways, each partner receives $75,000. Partner 1 receives $75,000 for his contribution of time, effort and expertise. Partners 2, 3, and 4 each earn $15,000 for their contribution of cash ($75,000 − $60,000 investment), which is a 25 percent return on their investment.

Three equal partners.   Figure 7-5 illustrates a variation in which three people with equal cash contributions of $50,000 get together to purchase a property for a total cash outlay of $150,000. They each put an additional $10,000 into repairs and then sell the property for $300,000. In this case, the total individual contribution of $60,000 earns each partner $100,000, or a profit of $40,000.

Other partnership options.   You will need to decide whether you are interested in a long-term partnership (where you and your partners rent out the property to tenants for an agreed-upon period of time before you sell it) or a short-term partnership (where you and your partners fix up the property and resell it for a profit soon after you purchase it). Another partnership option could be to allow one of the partners to refinance and buy out the other partners. Equity sharing (see Chapter 8) is yet another form of a partnership—one that pairs owner-occupants with investors.

A realistic and accurate knowledge of the market is crucial to the success of any partnership. People who wish to form partnerships to purchase foreclosures are strongly advised to seek the advice of financial advisors who can help them plan the best partnership arrangements for their financial goals and an attorney who can help develop a contract that clearly defines each partner's duties, roles, intentions, goals, and so on.

Category 3: Foreclosure Purchasers with a Lot of Cash and Good Credit

People in Category 3 who wish to purchase foreclosures should consider these alternatives.

All of the Above Plus . . .

If you have cash and good credit, you have the advantage of being able to purchase foreclosures using any of the strategies recommended to the people in Category 1 and Category 2. Your access to cash and credit also provides you with some additional creative options.

Buy Foreclosures with Cash at the Auction

You can purchase foreclosures with cash, fix them up, and flip (sell) them to someone else for a profit. Or if you want to keep the property as an investment and rent it out to tenants, you can purchase the property at the auction with cash, fix it up, and obtain financing from a bank later. Your advantage is that you have the financial resources to keep the property while it builds equity. The downside is that if you don't do your "homework" and purchase a property safely and sanely, it can cost you money instead of making you money.

Buy Foreclosures in Bulk from Banks and Government Agencies

You can also use your resources of cash and credit to your advantage if you buy more than one property at a time. In this situation you can offer to pay cash as a down payment on several properties, with the bank or government agency providing financing for the balance of the purchase price. The benefit is that you can get discounts on the prices of the properties when you purchase them in bulk. The downside is the expense of the closing costs for multiple properties. But this cost can be offset by taking one blanket loan on all of the properties and incorporating a "release clause" into the loan terms for any property that you sell off. Here is an example of how it works.

You purchase four properties for $600,000, put down $100,000 as a down payment, and get a loan for the remaining $500,000. You allocate the loan to the four properties in accordance with their values. In this example let's assume that all four properties have similar values, and the purchase prices will be allocated equally at $150,000. The down payment of $100,000 is also allocated equally, $25,000 to each property. The remaining balance of $125,000 for each of the four properties ($150,000 purchase price less the $25,000 down payment) is financed through the bank, but instead of having four different loans and four separate closings and costs, you have one blanket loan for $500,000 (and one closing) with a release clause that requires a payment of $125,000 to the lender when each property is sold. This means that instead of the entire loan coming due if one property is sold, each property can be sold off independently, and the blanket loan remains intact for the rest of the loans. So in two years, if you sell one of the properties for $200,000, you pay off the "release" amount that was allocated, in the amount of $125,000 to the bank, and the remaining $75,000 is your profit. The new balance remaining on the loan is reduced by the $125,000 you have just paid off. The remaining loan balance of $375,000 less the monthly loan payments you have been making will be reduced further each time another property is sold off.

Category 4: Foreclosure Purchasers with a Lot of Cash and Tarnished Credit

People in Category 4 who wish to purchase foreclosures should consider these alternatives:

Finance with a Partner

If a lender will give you financing, but it would be expensive because of your poor credit history, you may be able to remedy the problem by purchasing with a partner who has good credit. This way, you can at least obtain financing for your initial purchase. As you make your payments in a timely fashion, you continue to repair your credit until you can eventually qualify for financing on your own. In your partnership agreement, you can arrange in advance to buy out your partner at a predetermined date in the future if you really want to keep the property, or you can sell the property and use your share of the proceeds as a down payment on a different property.

Earn a Better Rate

You may be able to find a lender that will agree—in writing—to renegotiate a prearranged lower rate of interest after you have proven yourself by making timely payments for an agreed-upon period of time (e.g., your rate will be adjusted after three years of timely payments).

Purchase with Cash Now and Finance Later

You can use your cash to help you reestablish credit.

If all else fails and you are unable to find a lender to finance the property, another option is to buy the foreclosure with cash and obtain financing down the road, after you have reestablished your credit in other ways (e.g., through a secured credit card). Consult a credit counselor who can help you define a plan of action to repair your credit in a time frame that is compatible with your investing goals.

8

Equity Sharing:
Buying Foreclosures
with a Partner

Equity sharing is a creative approach to buying foreclosures with a partner, sharing the benefits derived from that partnership during the term of the agreement, and splitting the profits after the property is sold and the partnership term ends.

In Chapter 8, we revisit the partnership concept from Chapter 7 and apply it to two circumstances in which equity sharing strongly benefits the participants. The first arrangement is between parents and children, and the second arrangement is between investors and contractors.

Please note that the prices in Chapter 8 are for demonstration purposes only—in some parts of the country, housing prices for residential properties and housing costs, including property taxes and homeowner's insurance, are lower than the numbers set forth in this chapter. Conversely, in other parts of the country, these prices will be higher.

How It Works

An equity-sharing arrangement involves two partners. One partner is the *inside occupant*; the other partner is the *outside investor*. The inside occupant lives in the house and generally contributes less money toward purchasing and financing the premises and more toward the monthly expenses. The outside investor does not live in the house and generally contributes less money toward the monthly expenses and more toward purchasing and financing the property.

For the purposes of the equity-sharing arrangements that are discussed in this chapter, each of the partners owns a 50 percent interest in the property, and both partners have their names on the financing and ownership documents (note, loan, deed of trust, and so on).

Equity sharing is based on the premise that real estate will appreciate in value over time. It is implemented most effectively in a rising real estate market.

Why It Works

In order to appreciate fully the benefits that equity sharing brings to those involved, we must first understand each party's goals and the challenges that each party faces in trying to achieve them.

The Owner-Occupant's Goals and Challenges

The Goals

The two main objectives for home buyers are, first, to purchase a home for their families to live in for many years to come, thereby attaining "the American Dream of homeownership," and, second, to finance their "American Dream" with a loan that they can afford to pay every month.

The Challenges

In today's residential real estate market, property taxes, high interest rates, and costly housing prices can cause the "American Dream" to remain an elusive fantasy for many people. In addition, escalating rental prices prevent many tenants from saving enough money to buy their own homes. Traditionally, a buyer needs enough cash for a 10 percent down payment and, depending on the financing practices in the state in which the property is located, anywhere from 3 to 5 percent of the loan amount for closing costs. When people without substantial financial resources strive to acquire a home of their own, these challenges often appear to be insurmountable.

The Investor's Goals and Challenges

The Goals

In order to address the problems faced by today's real estate investors, we must understand their main objectives. An investor is someone who purchases real estate at a below-market price, without any intention of occupying it as a primary dwelling, using as little of his or her own money as possible (meaning that investors use "other people's money," namely, bank money). Investment property can be either "income-producing" (where the "income produced" is the monthly rental amount paid by the tenant to the landlord) or "non-income-producing" (where no income is produced, but the property is a second home and/or a vacation home). For equity sharing purposes in this chapter, the investment property will be income producing.

An investor typically buys the property either to fix up and resell quickly (fix and flip) or to hold for a number of years and rent it out to tenants during that time.

When an investor becomes a landlord, he or she maintains ownership of the property, and the tenant pays a monthly rent payment that covers all, or if not all most, of the investor's monthly loan payment. The investor benefits because the rent income is used to cover the monthly loan payment, which, in turn, reduces the balance of the outstanding loan and builds equity for the investor. With careful planning, at some point in the future the property will be sold, and the proceeds will provide a source of liquid funds to help finance the investor's retirement. There are, however, certain aspects of owning income-producing rental property that can be financially troubling for inexperienced investors who become landlords.

The Challenges

Problems with tenants   When investors rent out property to others, they become landlords. Problems can arise if the investors do not take their responsibilities as landlords seriously. The most common problem that investors encounter is that tenants violate their lease agreements. Being a landlord requires much more than just collecting the rent and paying the loan each month. Typical headaches for landlords include the following:

Vacancies.   The loan payment comes out of the landlord's pocket if there are no tenants living in the property and paying the rent.

Repair costs.   Inexperienced landlords may have a lease that does not protect them properly when disputes arise with their tenants.

Tenant turnover.   Depending on the length of tenancy specified in the lease, there may be a yearly turnover of tenants, which may require a new paint job, interior and exterior cleaning, and costly advertising expenses.

Rent collection.   The tenants may have a problem paying their rent on time—or at all!

Deadbeat tenants.   Unless a landlord is experienced in screening prospective tenants, he or she runs the risk of renting to a "deadbeat" tenant who refuses to pay the rent and who damages the rental property.

Problems with the high cost of loans for investors

High interest rates.   From a lender's standpoint, there are two classifications of property owners: owner-occupants who use the property as their primary dwelling, and investors who are non-owner-occupants and use the premises as a rental property or a vacation home. Interest rates for investor loans are almost always higher than interest rates for owner-occupant loans because there is a greater risk factor involved. Why? When an applicant applies for a loan on a property that he or she will be living in, the lender's qualifying process ensures that the applicant who will be occupying the premises has the financial capability to repay the loan each month. On the other hand, when an investor purchases a property to rent out to tenants, the lender's qualifying process extends only to the investor, not to the tenants who will be occupying the premises, and the lender has no control over the manner in which the investor qualifies the tenants. Although many lenders take the anticipated rental income (or a percentage thereof) into consideration when calculating the investor's income-to-debt ratio during the qualification process, if the investor leases the property to tenants who do not pay their rent and the investor is unable to carry the financing costs without that rental income, the loan on the rental property could end up in default. Thus, banks offset the investor's greater risk of default by charging higher interest rates and more points for loans on investment properties, and this, in turn, increases the monthly expenses and, in many cases, eliminates the expectation of a positive cash flow.

Negative cash flow. Cash flow is the money that "flows" into and out of a rental property. A positive cash flow is achieved when the income flowing into the property exceeds the expenditures flowing out of the property. A negative cash flow results when expenditures exceed income.

For example, let's say that we are looking for a foreclosure to purchase as an investment property and that we intend to rent it out to tenants. As part of our preliminary preparations, we perform a cash flow analysis (see "Calculating Cash Flow" in Chapter 9). We subtract the carrying charges and expenses flowing out of the property (i.e., the loan payment, property taxes, and property insurance), in this case totaling $1,550 per month, from the rental income of $1,500 per month flowing into the property, and we can project a negative cash flow of approximately $50 per month.

Monthly rent income:	$1,500.00	per month
Monthly expenses:	(1,550.00)	per month
Negative cash flow:	($ 50.00)	per month

A 25 percent down payment requirement. Another big headache for investors is the 25 percent down payment that lenders require for a loan approval. By contrast, the owner-occupant can get financing with as little as 5 to 10 percent down (and even less with some government-backed loans). Once again, this is tied to the greater risk factor for loans on investment rental properties. Remember, investors do not like to use their own money, and the substantially higher cash outlay that they are required to make can be an insurmountable hurdle.

Comparing Purchase Details and Finance Costs

Figure 8-1 compares and contrasts the differences in the purchasing details and financing costs when owner-occupants buy property to live

COMPARING PURCHASES DETAILS:
OWNER-OCCUPANT, INVESTOR, AND
EQUITY-SHARING PARTNERS

	As Owner-Occupant	As Investor	As Equity-Sharing Partners
Financing the loan:			
Interest rate (%)	7%	10%	7%
Purchase price	$300,000	$300,000	$300,000
Less: down payment	(30,000)—10%	(75,000)—25%	(30,000)—10%
Financing required	$270,000	$225,000	$270,000
Cash required:			
Down payment	$30,000	$75,000	$30,000
Add: closing costs (5%)	$13,500	$11,250	$13,500
Total cash required	$43,500	$86,250	$43,500
Monthly loan costs:			
Loan amount	$270,000/30 yr	$225,000/30 yr	$270,000/30 yr
Interest rate	7%	10%	7%
Principal and interest	$ 1,796	$ 1,975	$ 1,796
Property taxes	$ 416	$ 416	$ 416
Property insurance	$ 100	$ 100	$ 100
Mortgage insurance premium (MIP)	$ 100	$ 0	$ 100
Monthly loan payment	$ 2,412	$ 2,491	$ 2,412
Monthly cash flow:			
Rental income	$ 0	$ 1,500	$ 2,412
Less: carrying	$ 0	(2,491)	(2,491)
Monthly cash flow	$ 0	$ (991)	($ 0)

Figure 8-1. Owner-occupant, investor, and equity-sharing partners—comparing purchase details.

in, when investors buy property to rent out to tenants, and when these parties form a partnership to purchase under an equity-sharing arrangement. As a reminder, the numbers in this chapter are for demonstration purposes only. The factors for these purchases are as follows:

Purchase price:	$300,000
Yearly property taxes:	$ 5,000
Projected monthly rental income:	$ 1,500

The subject property in Figure 8-1 is being purchased for $300,000. The yearly property taxes are $5,000, and the projected rental income is $1,500 per month. The monthly loan payment includes the loan principal and interest, and the loan will be fully amortized over 30 years.

Interest Rate

In comparing an owner-occupant versus investor situation, we have an owner-occupant who is paying a 7 percent interest rate compared to an investor who is paying a higher rate of 10 percent. *Advantage: Owner-occupant*

Earnings

Because he is required to put a lower percent down, and therefore requires a larger loan, the owner-occupant needs a higher annual income than the investor. *Advantage: Investor*

Down Payment

The owner-occupant is traditionally required to make a lower down payment (only 10 percent compared to 25 percent for the investor). *Advantage: Owner-occupant*

Closing Costs

The closing costs in Figure 8-1 include the owner-occupant's attorney fees, escrow charges for taxes and insurance, title fees, appraisal fees, and the bank attorney fees, as well as other ordinary closing costs. Closing costs vary from state to state, but in this example the 5 percent applies to both the owner-occupant and the investor.

The owner-occupant needs a total of $43,500 to complete the transaction. This includes the 10 percent down payment of $30,000 plus closing costs of $13,500 (estimated as 5 percent of the $270,000 loan). The investor needs a total of $86,250 for this transaction. This amount includes the 25 percent down payment of $75,000 plus closing costs of $11,250 (estimated at 5 percent of the $225,000 loan). *Advantage: Owner-occupant*

Monthly Loan Payment

The owner-occupant's monthly payment will also initially include private loan insurance costs also known as a mortgage insurance premium (MIP) of approximately $100 per month, since the purchaser is putting down less than 20 percent to purchase the property. The total monthly cost to the owner-occupant is $2,412. *Advantage: Investor*

Summary of Costs for the Owner-Occupant

The owner-occupant will pay a lower interest rate than the investor but must pay an additional amount each month to cover the private loan insurance. The owner-occupant must save the formidable sum of $43,500 for the down payment and closing costs and must show enough income to qualify for a $270,000 loan.

Summary of Costs for the Investor

The investor will pay a higher interest rate than the owner-occupant, but will not have to pay private loan insurance because of his 25 percent down payment. The investor, however, must come up with $86,250 for the down payment and closing costs, and must show enough income to qualify for a $225,000 loan.

So What Do We Have?

We have an owner-occupant who must try to save $43,500 and hope that by the time he does so, housing costs will not have increased beyond his price range. We have an investor who does not want to use his own cash, but who, nevertheless, must come up with almost twice as much money as the owner-occupant, and, to add insult to injury, the investor will suffer a negative cash flow in excess of $900 a month!

Equity Sharing to the Rescue

Equity sharing eliminates many of the aforementioned problems faced by home buyers and investors. When two individuals buy a property as co-owners under an equity-sharing agreement, they each get the best of both worlds. How? By seamlessly bridging the gap between the investor's need for "affordable financing" and the owner-occupant's quest for "affordable housing."

The Inside Occupant

The inside occupant (we'll call this partner the "insider") can now achieve home ownership for a much smaller cash outlay than if he or she purchased the property individually because the insider's partner, the outside investor, will contribute the largest share (maybe all) of the down payment and closing costs.

The Outside Investor

The outside investor (we'll call this partner the "investor") can still retain the income tax benefits but loses the "high-risk" stigma that caused the high loan costs because the investor's co-owner, the insider, will live in the house. Also, tenant problems and overall risk are minimized because the tenant is also an owner.

As illustrated in Figure 8-1, each partner receives the benefit of the other partner's advantages while eliminating the risks and expenses that had been so problematic. A new, more favorable financial picture begins to emerge.

Interest Rate

The investor now shares the benefit of the lower interest rate that was previously available only to the owner-occupant (7 percent instead of 10 percent), since his or her partner (the insider) will live in the house.

Earnings

The insider does not have to earn as much income to qualify for the loan because the investor is now a co-borrower, and his or her income is combined with the insider's during the income qualifying process.

Down Payment

The investor gets the benefit of the insider's lower down payment requirement—10 percent instead of 25 percent—because this purchase is no longer considered an investment. Since one of the partners (the insider) will be living in the house, equity sharing gives both partners the insider's owner-occupant status. Remember, investors like to use as little of their own money as possible!

Negative Cash Flow

Negative cash flow for the investor is eliminated, since the insider's "rent" each month will pay the carrying charges on the property.

Contract Terms to Agree Upon

As I said earlier, the beauty of equity-sharing arrangements is in the flexibility of the terms of the agreement. Each party should consult with an attorney, an accountant, and/or a financial advisor to ensure that each partner's needs are provided for. The following are some of the terms to consider.

The Purchase Price Limits

The price of the property to be purchased must be determined and agreed to initially by both the insider and the investor, since the partners will be co-owners.

The Percent of Down Payment and Closing Cost Contributions

The insider and the investor must agree to the portion of the down payment and closing costs that each party will contribute. In some cases, the investor agrees to pay the entire down payment and closing costs, and in other cases, the partners agree to a 50-50 split, in which each partner pays 50 percent of the amounts needed. Also commonly used is a 60-40 split, in which the investor pays 60 percent of the down payment and closing costs and the insider pays 40 percent. A 70-30 split, an 80-20 split, and a 90-10 split are also popular arrangements.

Figure 8-2 illustrates a 90-10 split, in which the investor contributes 90 percent of the down payment and closing costs and the insider contributes 10 percent. The purchase price is set at $300,000, and a 10 percent down payment of $30,000 is required. Total closing costs are estimated at 5 percent of the $270,000 financed, or $13,500. The total down payment and closing costs for both partners to split, $30,000 + $13,500, is $43,500. In this example of a 90-10 split, the investor will pay 90 percent of $43,500, which amounts to $39,150, and the insider will pay 10 percent of $43,500, which amounts to $4,350. Now compare these numbers to the total amount each would have had to pay without equity sharing: the investor's required cash outlay plummeted from $86,250 to $43,500, and the insider's cash outlay fell from $43,500 to $4,350.

EQUITY SHARING ARRANGEMENT—90-10 SPLIT

Purchase price	$300,000
Down payment required	$ 30,000 (*10% of purchase price*)
Financing required	$270,000
Closing costs required	$ 13,500 (*5% of loan*)

	Investor*	Insider*
Down payment contribution	$ 27,000	$ 3,000
Closing cost contribution	+ 12,150	+ 1,350
Total cash contribution required	$ 39,150	$ 4,350

*Investor contributes 90 percent and insider contributes 10 percent of the down payment and closing costs.

Figure 8-2. A 90 percent/10 percent split under an equity-sharing arrangement.

The agreed-upon contributions for the down payment and the closing costs do not have to be the same percentage. For instance, the agreement may call for a 90-10 split toward the down payment, but the two parties will contribute equally (a 50-50 split) toward the closing costs.

The Contribution for the Monthly Carrying Charges

In some cases, the partners agree that the carrying charges (payment of loan principal and interest, property taxes, and property insurance) will be treated as the insider's monthly rent. This means that the insider will pay the total monthly loan costs for the property. Again, there are no hard-and-fast rules about the way the carrying charges are split. It may be agreed that the insider and the investor will share the carrying charges equally. Internal Revenue Service regulations may require that the insider pay what would be considered fair market "rent" to the investor for using the half of the house that the investor owns, since technically both partners own the property and the insider is occupying both his or her half and the investor's half.

In some cases, the IRS may disallow some of the income tax deductions taken by either party unless "fair market rent" is paid. For this reason and many others, the partners should each seek expert advice so that the entire equity-sharing arrangement is structured to fit their individual financial circumstances.

The Amount of Homeowner's Insurance Coverage

Both partners must agree to purchase a homeowner's insurance policy to protect their interests (and the lender's interest) in the property. There are many variations of policies to select from, and the partners should seek the advice of a homeowner's insurance expert.

The Amount of Life Insurance Coverage

The partners should agree to purchase a life insurance policy that covers the outstanding loan balance. If one of the partners dies, the loan can be paid off with the proceeds of the policy. The contract should also provide for the disposal of the property if one partner dies. For example, the agreement could direct that the property be sold to the public (or to the remaining partner) and the equity distributed between the deceased partner's estate and the surviving partner, pursuant to the disbursement provisions in the agreement.

How the Co-owners Will Own the Premises

To ensure that the property selection and ensuing agreement meet the future financial goals of the parties, each partner should seek advice from a financial expert and/or accountant and/or estate planner on how to form a business entity (e.g., forming a corporation or partnership), as well as how to select the percentage of ownership that will be held by each partner.

The Contribution toward Repairs and Other Cash Expenses

The following are some of the most common contribution variations:

1. Both partners share all cash expenses (monthly loan repairs, insurance, and property taxes).

2. The investor pays all cash expenses, and the insider pays a higher rent to cover the monthly cash expenses.

3. The insider pays all cash expenses and carrying charges, and the investor pays a larger portion of the down payment and closing costs.

The Income Tax Benefits

The IRS has established favorable income tax treatment for real estate investments. To ensure that both partners receive the maximum benefits from their equity-sharing arrangement, each party should be represented by financial experts or accountants with experience in equity-sharing agreements.

The Depreciation Deduction

In the context of this book, depreciation is an investment allowance associated with income taxes, which results from the decline in the value of real estate over time due to such factors as wear and tear and adverse changes to a neighborhood. The investor, who does not live in the house, is the only partner allowed the depreciation deduction.

The Interest Deduction

The agreement covering the split of the interest deduction on the loan for financing the property can be calculated in accordance with each partner's contribution during the year. For example, if each party contributes half of the loan payment, then each party may be able to claim 50 percent of the loan interest deduction.

The Payment of Operating Expenses

Usually the insider is responsible for expenses for utilities, such as heat, electricity, and water, since it is the insider who will live in the house and enjoy the benefit of the utilities.

The Split of the Equity When the Arrangement Ends

The value of the property above the loan balance is the partners' equity. One of the most important terms of an equity-sharing agreement is the allocation of that equity when the partnership terminates. This amount is often determined in conjunction with the contributions that each partner makes at the beginning of the partnership. For example, if each partner initially contributes 50 percent toward the down payment and closing costs, then the agreement may call for a 50-50 allocation of the equity that accumulates during the term of the partnership when the property is sold. If the value of the property is $350,000 when it is sold and the unpaid loan balance is $270,000, then the equity in the property is $80,000. In a 50-50 allocation, each partner would be entitled to $40,000. This same concept can be applied to the 90-10 split used in Figure 8-2. In that case, the investor would be entitled to 90 percent of the equity, and the insider would be entitled to 10 percent. Some agreements call for one or both partners to be reimbursed for their original outlay for the down payment and closing costs, after which the remaining equity is divided up according to the distribution percentages that were established.

The Market Value

An accurate market value of the property is essential to the partners when they buy the property, and again when they sell it. The manner in which the appraisals are ordered, the prices that the appraiser will charge, and the credentials of the appraisal company should be agreed to as part of the equity-sharing agreement. One arrangement is that both partners obtain independent reports from licensed appraisal firms and the property value is established by averaging the two appraisals.

The Termination Agreement

The equity-sharing agreement must provide for the venture to end. As stated previously, equity-sharing arrangements generally last for a term of one to five years. At that point, the equity-sharing agreement will be terminated through the contractual terms of a prearranged process.

A buy-out between partners   One approach is a buyout arrangement, where one of the partners buys out the other partner's interest in the property. The agreement should describe the method for determining the buyout amount, as well as the source of the funds that will be used to pay the agreed-upon amount. Will the buying partner have to obtain a new loan and pay off the original loan so that the selling partner is no longer a party to the original loan obligation? Will the buying party be able to keep the existing loan in place and pay off the other party with cash—and if so, will the lending institution release the selling partner from the loan obligation? These details are important, because if the selling partner's name is still on the loan documents, later on, if the buying partner defaults on the loan payments, the selling partner could be held responsible for the debt even though he or she is no longer an owner.

A public sale   If the termination agreement calls for the premises to be sold to someone other than either partner, these details should also be addressed in the agreement. For example, will the house be listed for sale exclusively with one particular real estate broker (an "exclusive" listing), or will it be offered through an "open" listing, where only the real estate broker who sells the property will earn the commission? Or will the partners try to market and sell the property themselves? Other decisions include the length of time that the listing will be given to a real estate broker and the commission rate to be paid.

Prevention against Future Borrowing

There should be some agreement between the insider and the investor that the property may not be used as collateral for any future loan that either partner obtains individually. The agreement should also prohibit a second lien on the property, since this could extinguish the equity that is accumulating.

Protection against Buyout
Option Defaults

There should be some stipulation in the contract about the consequences and expenses that will be incurred if the party who has agreed to buy out the other party fails to fulfill that obligation in good faith and in a timely fashion.

Payment Defaults

There should be an agreement as to the consequences that will ensue should either party default by failing to pay the carrying charges, loan payments, other expenses, and so forth.

Dispute Remedies

Both partners should agree to the manner in which they will settle disputes that may arise during the time that they are partners. The choices can include, but are not limited to, the use of arbitration boards and/or litigation through the court systems. The agreement can also include a provision whereby the defaulting party agrees to pay legal fees that result if the nondefaulting party must begin litigation to enforce his or her rights.

The Risks Involved in Equity Sharing

As with any endeavor that involves an investment of money, there are always risks. Since equity sharing relies on the premise that property values will appreciate, declining market prices are one potential risk.

However, because the need for housing continues to rise with the times, most experts feel that real estate will always be a viable investment over time.

If either partner defaults on the agreement, there is the chance that one partner may have to be responsible for the other partner's portion of the carrying charges, in addition to his or her own. The equity-sharing agreement may have to be terminated and the property sold, but both partners would still get the benefit of their share of the equity increase. As the term of ownership lengthens and equity accumulates, the risks to the partners diminish.

Equity Sharing for Parents and Children

The following example is one in which parents and their child wish to form an equity-sharing arrangement in order to purchase a foreclosure. The parents are looking for a tax shelter, and the child has a good income and can afford the monthly loan and carrying charges but has no cash saved up for the down payment and closing costs.

Let's say the parents and the child purchase an REO from a lending institution for $300,000. The property taxes are $5,000 per year. They put 10 percent down, and the lending institution has agreed to give them 90 percent financing for 30 years at a 7 percent interest rate. The parents will pay 100 percent of the down payment and closing costs. The child will pay all the monthly carrying charges and will be responsible for completing any repairs. The parents will get 100 percent of the depreciation as a tax benefit, and they will split the loan interest deduction 50-50 with the child. The parents and child will sell the property in five years and split the equity 50-50 after the sale. Figure 8-3 illustrates the way this will work.

After five years, the loan balance will be approximately $253,842. If the property appreciates at the rate of 4 percent per year and is sold for $364,990, the equity proceeds of $111,148 would give each of the partners (parents and child) $55,574 in a 50-50 split. In tabular format, this is:

Property value	$364,990 (4% appreciation yearly for five years)
Less: remaining loan balance	($253,842) (approximately)
Equity proceeds	$111,148
Split	$ 55,574 each

The parents earned $55,574 from their $43,500 investment, a profit of $12,074, which comes to approximately a 5 percent yearly return on

Equity-Sharing Arrangement between Parents and Child

Purchase price:	$300,000
Loan amount:	$270,000 (*7% interest for 30 years*)
Closing costs:	5% of $270,000 loan ($13,500)
Yearly property taxes:	$5,000
Down payment contribution:	100% (*paid by parents/investors*)
Closing cost contribution:	100% (*paid by parents/investors*)
Carrying charges:	100% (*paid by child/insider*)
Repairs:	100% (*paid by child/insider*)
Tax benefits:	Parents get depreciation
	Mortgage interest is split 50-50
Buyout time:	5 years
Equity split:	50-50

	Parents	Child
Initial purchase:		
Down payment	$30,000	–
Closing costs	3,500	–
Cash outlay	$43,500	–

	Parents	Child
Monthly carrying:		
Principal/interest	–	$1,796
Property taxes	–	$ 416
Property insurance	–	$ 100
MIP	–	$ 100
Total monthly carrying	–	$2,412

Figure 8-3. An equity-sharing arrangement between parents and their child.

their investment. They also benefited from the depreciation and loan interest deductions they claimed on their income tax returns.

The child will now have $55,574 to use as a down payment on another property and will hopefully be able to buy the next home on his or her own.

Equity Sharing for an Investor and a Contractor

Let's look at another type of equity-sharing arrangement, this time between a contractor and an investor. The contractor will be the insider, and will live in the house while making the repairs. The investor will be responsible for the initial cash outlay to cover the down payment and closing costs, and the contractor's contribution will be the repairs made to the property.

Unlike the equity-sharing arrangement between the parents and their child, where the partners must usually wait for their equity to accumulate over time, in the investor and contractor arrangement, the equity accumulation is accelerated because of renovation work that immediately improves the value of the property. Therefore, both partners usually agree to sell the property as soon as the repairs are completed.

In this case, the partnership agreement should clearly describe a list of the repairs that will be made by the contractor as his or her contribution, as well as the deadline for completing the work and the legal consequences and remedies that will arise if the work is not completed in a timely fashion. Another factor that should be confirmed is that the lender will not charge a prepayment penalty if the partners pay off the loan within the first couple of months after purchasing the house.

Finding a Partner for Equity Sharing

An Inside Occupant Who Is Looking for an Investor as a Partner Should Do the Following:

- Make an appointment with your attorney, your accountant, and/or your financial advisor to work out a plan that meets your present and future monetary goals.

- To attract investors, put an ad in your local newspaper, such as: "Ownership of income-producing property for sale at owner-occupant rates. Investor's dream: 90 percent profit when sold—0 percent headaches of being a landlord. Positive cash flow monthly. Call Mr. Insider at (000) 000-0000."

- Look in the classified section of your local newspaper under such headings as "Money to Lend." Investors with money for this sort of venture may advertise in this medium.

- When you find an investor to work with, set up an appointment to discuss your intentions and to outline a plan of action regarding the cost of the property you wish to purchase and the contribution you will be making. You will also need to structure the tax deductions, the monthly payment setup, the buyout terms, whether to form a business entity, and if so, what kind, and so on.

- Both partners should meet with their attorneys, accountants, and/or tax advisors to ensure that everyone's intentions are clear and everyone's interests are protected in a legally binding contract.

- Inspect and select the property that is right for you.

- File your loan application, close, and begin your new venture.

The Outside Investor Looking for an Insider as a Partner Should Do the Following:

- Consult your tax advisor or attorney to review the tax consequences of your role in equity sharing, as well as your capital requirements and availability of funds.

- Put an ad in your local newspaper to attract an insider, as follows: "Zero percent cash down buys 50 percent ownership of an eight-room high-ranch in Any County, USA. Payments each month equal rent of $____. No need to qualify for a home loan. Call Ms. Investor at (000) 000-0000."

- When you find an insider who will be your partner, it may be advisable to request a credit report to ensure that he or she will make a creditworthy partner.

- Outline a plan of action with the insider regarding the cost of the property you wish to purchase and the contribution you will be making. You will also need to agree on the tax deductions, the monthly payment setup, the buyout terms, whether to form a business entity, and if so what kind, and so on.

- Both partners should meet with their attorneys, accountants, and/or tax advisors to ensure that everyone's intentions are clear and everyone's interests are protected in a legally binding contract.

- Inspect and select the property that is right for you.
- File the loan application, close, and begin your new venture.

Equity Sharing Helps People Achieve Their Goals

Equity sharing satisfies the needs of an investor who wants to buy a foreclosure to use as a rental property with an owner-occupied (more favorable) interest rate and less costly carrying expenses, and who wants the added security of a good tenant who is also the coowner. It also satisfies the needs of a prospective home buyer who would like to purchase a foreclosure to live in, but who does not currently have the finances to do so independently.

9

Choosing the Right Property: What You Don't Know Can Hurt You

Most foreclosures are sold in "as-is" condition. This wording places buyers "on notice" that they are waiving the traditional warranties that the fixtures; appliances; heating, lighting, and electrical systems; and so on are in good working order that they might normally take for granted in traditional purchases. While an as-is condition disclaimer can leave foreclosure buyers vulnerable to "problem" properties, forewarned is also forearmed, and purchasers who are aware of their responsibility to protect their interests will (hopefully) be more diligent in their research and in calculating their expenses.

Ascertaining the condition of the property is just one of the preliminary preparations for selecting foreclosed properties. Chapter 9 introduces readers to the homework, legwork, and research skills that play an essential role in determining which properties are worth pursuing.

Finding the Right Property

You will need to inspect the properties that you are interested in, ask questions of certain people and agencies, and research the market conditions in your preferred locale before you attend any auctions or present any written offers to bank or government REO sellers or to defaulting borrowers. These preliminary preparations are the best way for you to uncover costly problems and to ensure accuracy in calculating the amount to pay for the property. The results of your inspections and research, combined with the answers to the questions in this chapter, will help you to more accurately distinguish a "dream" from a "disaster."

Getting Access

Your first step is to contact the referee, sheriff, or trustee, the foreclosing lender's attorney, the real estate broker, the homeowner, or another designated authority for access to the premises. You may be told, "You can inspect the property on Saturday at 3:00," or you may be told, "If you can get past the guy who lives there with the pit bull and the shotgun, be my guest!" In any event, be prepared to make your inspection.

The Preliminary Inspection

For inspection purposes, foreclosure properties are found in four basic conditions:

- *Vacant and accessible.* No one lives there, and you can go inside and inspect the premises.

- *Occupied and accessible.* Someone lives there and allows you inside to inspect the premises.

- *Vacant and inaccessible.* No one lives there, and there is no access to inspect the premises.

- *Occupied and inaccessible.* The unfriendly, angry occupant who lives there answers the door to greet you armed with his loaded shotgun and rabid pit bull and denies you access.

Keep in mind that the purpose of your inspection is to gather information that will help you identify potential problems and additional expenses when you calculate your bid limits. You will need to bring a pen or a pencil. (Forget about ballpoint pens in boarded-up houses in cold weather—the pens freeze and will not write properly.) Bring a camera for taking pictures of the properties, and a notepad for writing your observations about each property as you are performing your inspection. For efficiency and expediency, an instamatic or a digital camera that can provide you with an immediate image is recommended. (Imagine shooting an entire roll of film and finding out later that it didn't develop properly. Now, imagine how annoyed you will be when you have to go back and shoot everything all over again!) A flashlight or battery-operated lantern is also recommended if the house is vacant and the electrical system has been disconnected. Even if the electricity is working, you may still wish to illuminate areas within the property that are dimly lit in order to get a better view of the condition of the property. If you will be inspecting five or six properties, the most important thing you can do is to take specific notes about each one on a separate inspection form. You will never be able to remember all the details of each property unless you write down as much information as possible. To help you keep track of which notes go with which property, attach the pictures you take to each inspection sheet you prepare.

The important things to look at (in addition to the cosmetic appearance and the plumbing, heating, and electrical systems) are the structure itself; structural and cosmetic improvements, such as a shed, an in-ground pool, a detached new garage, and a second-story extension that looks like it was recently added; and anything else that may affect either the marketability or the value of the property.

Keep the pictures and the notes you have taken for later on, when you contact the various parties that are mentioned in this chapter. But first, I just want to give you a few words of advice before you perform your inspections.

Life-Saving Safety Tips for Inspections

No smoking. When you are inspecting vacant properties as part of your preliminary preparations for bidding, never enter a vacant house carrying a lighted cigarette. There may be a gas leak that no one is aware of (since no one lives there), and a lighted cigarette could cause an explosion of life-threatening proportions.

Don't go alone. Unlike traditional homes that are for sale, foreclosures are often vacant, and vacant houses can attract vandals or vagrants. Of even greater concern is the fact that the previous occupants may have left on unfriendly terms or in an irate state of mind. Here are two extreme examples that help illustrate this warning. In the first example, a student who attended one of my foreclosure seminars relayed an incident about a two-story vacant house where the previous owner, before he or she left, cut a hole in the middle of the living room floor on the second story and covered up the hole with a throw rug. If anyone had stepped on the carpet, he or she could have fallen through to the first floor. In the second example, I sent a contractor out to a house to inspect it and prepare an estimate, and he was shaken up (but, thankfully, unhurt) when he opened the back door to enter the house and an axe swung down. He was careful and had quick reflexes, but this is another example of the importance of being careful, and bringing someone with you when you inspect foreclosed properties.

Another benefit of bringing someone with you is that two people are more likely to notice and remember important details about the properties that you inspect. For the most efficient use of your time, bring your contractor and/or engineer with you, and ask them to give you written estimates for the repairs.

Protect yourself. Another tip is illustrated by my own personal experience. After we inspected a vacant foreclosure, my assistant noticed something on my clothes, and pointed it out to me. I looked down and saw hundreds of small dots all over my white skirt. (It's a good thing that it was summertime and I was wearing a light-colored skirt!) Then I realized that the itching I was feeling wasn't imaginary, and that those little dots were moving! Fleas! Hundreds of fleas all over me! It seemed at the time that the fleas were waiting for someone's legs to present themselves for dinner. If my assistant hadn't noticed something on my skirt, I would have infested my car, and, consequently, my home. Finding yourself in such a situation is a nightmare, and it can be especially dangerous for people who are allergic to fleabites. The point is, remember to bring insect repellent and to wear protective clothing (or at least put rubber bands around the bottom of your pants legs) in order to keep these or other annoying creatures from crawling under your garments.

Once Is Not Enough

I suggest that you visit the properties you are interested in at different times of the day and in different weather conditions. Does the property flood during a heavy rain? Is the area surrounding the property a local hangout for noisy teenagers? Is the property near a body of water that might cause flooding or other problems at high tide? One bank representative told me about an REO situated on a canal that had recently been repossessed by the bank he worked for. Potential purchasers came to inspect the property in the morning, liked it, and put down a deposit. When they came back later in the afternoon, the high tide from the morning was gone, and they found fish all over the front lawn and rescinded their offer!

Don't stop now; there are other things to look for. Is there a railroad line nearby, and when the train comes through, does it shake the pictures off the wall and transform the bath water into a whirlpool? Your inspections may result in some very disturbing findings or in great news that the property is worth pursuing.

For many people, another issue of concern in today's society is the presence of sexual predators. One highly regarded Web site is Familywatchdog.us, which was developed by John Walsh from *America's Most Wanted.*

Asking the Right Questions

Your physical inspection of the properties will provide you with a foundation to begin your calculations. The questions that follow can help you identify costly expenses and prevent costly mistakes.

Questions to Ask the Foreclosing Lender's Attorney; Referee, Sheriff, or Trustee; Real Estate Broker; Property Manager; or Other Designated Official

How do you obtain access to the properties in order to perform an inspection?
For access to properties that will be sold at upcoming auctions, contact the

foreclosing lender or referee, sheriff, or trustee. (The names are usually included in legal notices, commercial foreclosure lists, and other such documents.) *For access to bank-owned and government-owned foreclosures,* contact the real estate broker or the designated property manager. (Names and contact information are usually included in REO and government agency lists and advertisements.) *For access to preforeclosures,* contact the defaulting borrowers.

Are the utilities operating, and (in cold climates) has the plumbing system been winterized? Before approving financing, most lenders will send a bank representative (i.e., the bank appraiser, asset manager) to inspect the plumbing, heating, and electrical systems and confirm that these systems are in good working order. If, for example, the house is vacant and the plumbing system has been winterized to prevent frozen pipes (in colder climates), the system cannot be tested properly, and the loan may be delayed or denied. The seller may have to dewinterize the plumbing system so that the lender can complete its inspection. Similarly, the sellers may have to contact utility companies (i.e., electric and gas providers) and heating suppliers to have them restore services so that the related systems can also be inspected. Even if you are not expecting to obtain financing from a lender (i.e., you are paying cash at the auction), you still want to have the systems turned on to calculate the costs of any repairs that may be needed.

Has the house been boarded up? If the premises are vacant and boarded up (entry doors and window glass were removed and replaced with plywood to protect against vandalism), you will have to bring sufficient supplemental lighting devices (i.e., lanterns) to perform your inspection. (There is nothing darker—or, for that matter, colder—than a boarded-up house.) Another issue to address is the whereabouts of the entry doors and window glass that were removed. If the property is sold "as is," the new owner will most likely have to pay for replacing the doors and windows. Were they stored in the garage in the backyard? Or if the property is an REO, maybe the bank has a storage facility where the windows and doors were taken for safekeeping. In any event, unless the seller is willing to guarantee in writing that the doors and windows will be provided, the costs for replacing them at your expense should be included as part of your bid calculations.

What form of down payment is required? Contact the referee, sheriff, or trustee or the foreclosing lender's attorney and ask what form the down payment must be in. Whether you are purchasing a bank foreclosure at an auction, an REO from a lender or a government agency, or a preforeclosure from a defaulting borrower, the down payment generally must be in the form of a certified check, an attorney's check, a cashier's check, or a money order. The down payment should be kept in an escrow account until the closing.

When is the closing date?   If you are the high bidder at a foreclosure auction, you must complete the transaction within 30 days. On the other hand, if you are purchasing a foreclosure from a defaulting borrower or a bank or government REO and the bank that owns the property agrees to provide financing, then the closing date will be set once the financing is approved by the bank.

Will I lose my down payment if I fail to close?   If you purchased the property at a foreclosure auction and you are unable to close within the 30-day period stipulated in the referee, sheriff, or trustee's contract, in most cases, the down payment will not be refundable if the failure to close is the fault of the high bidder. But if the foreclosing lender is unable to close for some reason, there is a possibility that the down payment might be refunded. Reasons may include, but are not limited to, improper service of legal documents on the delinquent borrower at the time the foreclosure action first began, additional liens and judgments that have been discovered that were accidentally omitted from the upset price (which could cause the upset price to be substantially higher), or the foreclosing lender's inability to provide the necessary legal documents. If you are purchasing an REO from a bank or government agency or a preforeclosure from a defaulting borrower, down payment refunds will be dictated by the contract terms. If the down payment is refundable, you will also want to know how long it will take for you to recover your money.

Is the contract assignable?   Contract laws are state-specific, but in most states, contracts are automatically assignable unless there is wording in the contract that forbids assignment. Usually, contracts for the sale of real estate where the financing *is not* contingent upon the buyer's income and credit rating (i.e., he or she is buying with cash at an auction) can be assigned to another buyer, as long as that substituted buyer has enough cash to close. Even when the contract is assignable, however, the original party is still obligated to complete the transaction if the party to whom the contract was assigned fails to do so. By contrast, when a buyer is purchasing an REO from a lender's inventory and the lender is providing the financing or when the buyer is purchasing a preforeclosure from a defaulting borrower, the loan's approval is contingent upon the buyer's income and credit rating, and therefore the buyer's contract is unlikely to be assignable.

Who is responsible for the protection of the premises between the contract and closing dates?   The risk of loss is a statutory issue for each state to decide. In addition, insurance carriers must comply with the state's insurance statutes pertaining to vacancy exclusions. The vacancy exclusion clause in insurance policies excludes coverage for properties that have been vacant for a stated period of time (i.e., 30 or 60 days). This means that the insurance company will not be liable for losses to a property that is vacant beyond that stipulated time frame. In many cases, however, the foreclosing lender cannot protect the premises or give any guarantees about its condition if there are people (i.e., the defaulting borrower or a tenant) occupying the property. If the property is vacant, however, the foreclosing lender's insurance policy may or may not cover any additional damages to the premises that occur between contract and closing.

Who is responsible for major structural repairs?   If you are purchasing the property at an auction, in most cases, you are responsible. Remember, you are purchasing the property in as-is condition. If you are purchasing an REO or a property that is owned by a government agency, however, you may be able to get financial assistance for repairs. I was once involved with an REO purchase in which the bank that owned it issued a $500 credit at the closing so that the purchaser could use that money to help repair a collapsed cesspool.

What is the status of the current occupants?   If you are the highest bidder at an auction and there are people currently living in the property, you will probably be responsible for the eviction procedures once you are the new owner. Sometimes the occupants have already advised the foreclosing lender that they will be moving out voluntarily. This may help you to be more accurate when you prepare your bid amount because you will know whether or not you can eliminate eviction costs from your bid calculations. If you are purchasing an REO from a lender's inventory, the property may have already been vacated. Some lenders with REOs in their inventories evict the occupants as a prerequisite to putting the property on the market. See Chapter 11 on negotiating with friendly or unfriendly occupants.

Is prepossession allowed prior to closing if you are in contract?   Ask if prepossession is allowed during the period of time between the contract and the closing. If the premises are vacant, you may want to begin making repairs in order to rent the property to tenants or to resell it more quickly than if you waited until after the closing. On the other hand, if you plan to live in the property and it is in good enough condition, you may want to move in yourself. Prepossession may also be granted by lending institutions for their REOs. The lending institutions may find this to be beneficial, especially when the property is vacant, as a means of avoiding vandalism.

There are some issues that may arise in connection with prepossession. In some cases, the seller may want you to pay "rent" for the period of time from the date you take possession up until the closing date. In that case, you will have to weigh the benefits you would gain from prepossession against the rental expense.

Some attorneys advise sellers and purchasers against prepossession because of the risk that something could go wrong during the financing and title processes that could interfere with the closing and invalidate the sale (e.g., financing is denied, unexpected title problems arise, and so on). In that situation, unless there was a specific provision in the contract terms to repay the prepossessor for labor and materials, it may be difficult, if not impossible, for you to recover any payment for repair costs that you incurred. If you are interested in prepossession, you should consider incorporating a repayment agreement into the contract whereby the seller agrees to pay you a preagreed price for completing specific work in the event that the closing is called off.

After both parties sign the contract, the purchaser, by virtue of having made the down payment, has an insurable interest in the property. Whereas you would normally expect to obtain property insurance that is effective on the day of the closing, if you are granted permission to take possession prior to closing, a crucial part of your rental agreement with the seller would be to ensure that the premises are covered against losses. Many times, you will be required to provide your own property insurance coverage that is effective on the date you are taking prepossession.

Does the foreclosed owner's "right of redemption" survive the auction? In a foreclosure action in some states, the previous owner's right of redemption is extinguished once the bidding begins. In other states, the owner's right of redemption may survive the auction, which means that even after the property is awarded to the highest bidder, for a limited period of time, the previous owner can still pay the upset price and redeem ownership of the premises.

Are there any additional liens or judgments attached to the premises? Ask if there are any additional liens or judgments attached to the premises for which you would be held responsible, in addition to the purchase price. This question is especially important in auction situations, where a diligent search of the public records in the county clerk's office is an essential preliminary preparation for uncovering liens that may be in a senior position and require payment in full when you become the new owner. By contrast, in most REO cases, the bank clears the title once the property comes back into its inventory by paying off the outstanding liens and judgments.

Questions to Ask the Town/City Hall (Where the Foreclosure Is Located)

Is there an existing certificate of occupancy (or its equivalent) on file? Contact (or visit) the town hall (or appropriate government agency) in the town where the property is located, and ask for a copy of the latest certificate of occupancy (also known as a "CO") that is on file there. A certificate of occupancy (or its equivalent) is issued by a town's (or another government agency's) building department and certifies that the construction of the dwelling was done in accordance with local building codes. An example of a certificate of occupancy is included as Figure 9-1.

Is there an updated survey on file?   Contact or visit the building department (or appropriate government agency) in the town where the property is located and ask for a copy of the latest survey that is on file there. A survey is an illustration of the property description. Figure 9-2 is an example of a survey for a property that was improved with a two-story dwelling.

Now compare your pictures from your preliminary property inspection to the certificate of occupancy and the survey. Make sure that all additional structures are accounted for. Sure, you may have always dreamed of that in-ground pool, and the deck that was added may look pretty sturdy, but if these improvements violate the building codes in your area or if they have not yet been inspected and approved by the property authorities, you could be in for some costly problems. In most states, a certificate of occupancy or its equivalent, along with an updated survey, is required in order for you to obtain a bank loan to purchase the premises. Even if you are buying the property at the auction with cash, and you don't need a loan, or if the REO seller agrees to "waive" the certificate of occupancy or survey and sell the property to you anyway, this is a sign of "deferred maintenance" rather than a favor. Why? When you try to sell the property in the future, whomever you sell the property to in later years will probably need a loan and will be unable to get one unless these documents can be produced. This may prove to be a costly undertaking if the improvements were never properly constructed and need to be redone.

Even when a foreclosure is missing these necessary documents, there are foreclosure purchasers who will still bid on the property (i.e., a cash purchaser who does not have to borrow money to purchase the foreclosure and is therefore exempt from meeting any lender's guidelines requiring a C of O, a survey, or the like or an REO purchaser when the REO seller provides financing and waives the C of O and/or survey requirement). When calculating their bid sheets, these purchasers take into consideration the costs that they will incur to obtain these documents, especially if legalizing the improvements and obtaining the documents costs $10,000 and the value of the property increases by $20,000–$30,000. For example, let's say you are interested in property that has an in-ground pool, but the previous owners never applied for the proper permits, and there is no certificate of occupancy to confirm that the pool was built in accordance with local building codes. While this situation seems like it could be highly problematic, your preliminary

BUILDING DEPARTMENT
TOWN OF SMITHTOWN
SUFFOLK COUNTY, N.Y.

CERTIFICATE OF OCCUPANCY

COMPLIANCE

This certifies that the ....Building...............................

located at S/S New Highway, Valmont Village, Sec. # 5 ....

....

....

Described .... Map No. .... Block .... Lot No..............

Conforms substantially with the terms and requirements of the New York State Building Code and

Town of Smithtown Zoning Ordinance, as amended to date, and may be permitted to be used and

occupied as a . One Family Dwelling 43.6 x 24.8 with 2 car att/garage ....

Subject to the following conditions: ....

....

....

Owner Melody Construction, Inc. Commack, NY.......................................

Signed ..... Harvey R. Manuel

BUILDING OFFICIAL

The building or any part there of shall not be used for any purposes other than for which it is certified. Cerficate will be null and void if this building is altered in any manner or additions are made thereto without authorization from the Building Department.

Figure 9-1. A certificate of occupancy.

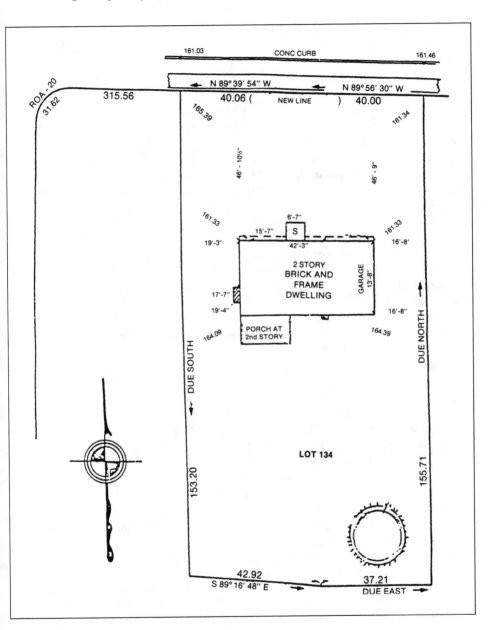

Figure 9-2. A survey.

preparations for determining whether or not to pursue this property can be broken down into four steps. First, arrange to meet the local building inspector (or whoever is in charge of issuing these documents) at the property, so that you can ascertain what specific repairs will be required (e.g., fences, electrical work, and so forth) to satisfy the building codes so that the certificate of occupancy can be issued for the pool. Second, get a written estimate from a licensed contractor for any repairs that you would have to complete to bring the pool into compliance with local building codes. Third, contact the local property tax collector to find out if there will be a significant increase in the property taxes once the improvements are completed and the certificate of occupancy is issued. Fourth, get a price from a surveyor for preparing an updated survey or any other documents required by the building department authorities to legalize the in-ground pool.

Many people feel that purchasing a property for a fraction of its actual value is financially beneficial, especially where legalizing an improvement worth $20,000–$30,000 only costs $10,000, even if some legwork is required to research and obtain the missing documents.

Does the local government require a rental permit for you to rent out the property that you are interested in, and is there a rental permit currently in effect? Some government zoning agencies require the owner of a rental property (yes, even a small single-family rental property) to obtain a rental permit before tenants can move in. The procedure may simply involve filing an application with the local building department and paying an annual (or biannual) rental permit fee. A physical inspection by a building inspector or other building official may also be required to ensure that the premises that are being rented out are fit for human habitation. Because procedures vary from location to location, investors should contact the local zoning authorities for information about the procedure that is followed in the area in which they wish to purchase foreclosures.

Are there any private deed or public zoning restrictions that could affect the current or future use of the premises by new owners or their tenants? Here are some examples of private deed restrictions or public zoning restrictions that could cause problems for future owners.

- A town with a rental permit requirement could pose a problem if the town has called a moratorium (a temporary halt) on issuing rental permits and you want to purchase an investment property in that town to rent out to tenants.

- There could be a restriction that prohibits owners of commercial vehicles from parking these vehicles (e.g., contractors, truck drivers) on the premises. This could cause problems if you drive a commercial vehicle, because you would have to find an alternative place to park it when you are not working, and will need to own a noncommercial vehicle to get back and forth from your home to the place where you park your commercial vehicle each day. If you plan to purchase the foreclosure as an investment to rent out to tenants, you would be limiting your tenant base if you were prevented from renting to tenants with commercial vehicles.

- There could be a restriction that controls the color and type of paint that must be used to repaint the exterior of the house, and you may not happy with any of the colors that you can choose from.

- In older homes, there could be a restriction on changing the exterior of the house if the premises are designated as a landmark of historical significance.

- There could be a private easement that allows a neighboring owner to use the property you are interested in purchasing for access to and from his landlocked residence.

Questions to Ask the Utility Companies (That Service the Premises)

Are there currently any outstanding utility debts? Contact the utility companies that service the premises (for example, water, gas, and electricity companies) and ask if there are any current outstanding utility debts. If there are, ask who is responsible for payment. Would you, as the new owner, have to pay off the arrears in order to reinstate service? The amount due may be substantial or it may be negligible, but in either case, knowing this amount will help you figure out your bid amount, since you will be incorporating all of your expenses into your final calculations.

Are there any incomplete community services? If you are purchasing property with an incomplete sewer hookup, you may run into a huge expense if the property is located a lengthy distance from the main sewer line connection. The same situation may occur in areas where well water is being replaced with city or community water services. If you are able to purchase the property for a low enough price, just incorporate the amount you will need for completing the hookup into your bid amount.

Organizing Yourself

Figure 9-3 is a checklist that you can use as a framework for the questions you will need to ask about the properties you are interested in. You may need to obtain additional information from other sources.

Prebid Questions

Foreclosing Lender's Attorney/Referee, Sheriff, or Trustee/Real Estate Broker/Designated Authority:

- Is the property vacant or occupied?
- If occupied, by whom?
- What is the status of the present occupants (i.e., staying, leaving, evicting)?
- Will there be access to the premises for inspection before bidding?
- What is the status of the utilities (heating, electric, and so on)?
- Has the plumbing system been winterized?
- Has the house been boarded up?
- If it is boarded up, where are the doors and windows that were removed?
- What form must the down payment be in?
- When is the required closing date?
- Will I lose my down payment if I fail to close?
- Is the contract assignable?
- Who is responsible for protection of the premises?
- Are there any credits given (off the sales price) for major structural repairs?
- Is prepossession allowed prior to closing?
- Are there any additional liens or judgments attached to the premises?

Building Department (Where the Premises Are Located):

- Is there a certificate of occupancy (or its equivalent) available?
- Is there an updated survey available?
- Is there a rental permit requirement for the township?
- Is there a current rental permit on file?
- Are there private or zoning restrictions that affect future owners?

Utility Companies (That Service the Premises):

- Are there currently any outstanding utility debts?
- Who is responsible for paying these outstanding utility debts?
- Are there any incomplete services (such as sewer or city water hookups)?

PLEASE NOTE: NOT ALL-INCLUSIVE—ADDITIONAL INFORMATION MAY BE REQUIRED

Figure 9-3. A sample checklist of prebid questions.

This checklist is not intended to be all-inclusive, and you should customize and supplement the list with additional tasks you must complete in accordance with your specific purchasing strategy.

Inspecting the File of the Foreclosure Action

If you are interested in purchasing preforeclosures from defaulting borrowers and properties at foreclosure auctions, contact the designated authority handling the foreclosure action and ask about access to the files that are part of the action. In most cases, these files are public records that are open for examination by the public at large. Most of the time, these files are stored somewhere in the county center in the county where the property is located. Files may be requisitioned by index number or some other identifying code that each public records bureau uses to distinguish one foreclosure from another. That index number or code usually appears in the legal notices that are publicized as part of the foreclosure procedure.

Hiring a Title Expert

Many people without experience in real estate title work feel unsure of their ability to ascertain that the property they are interested in is really a good choice. If you feel intimidated about asking questions or if you feel unsure of yourself and lack confidence in your ability to do the preliminary investigation work that's required, I strongly recommend that you hire a title (or foreclosure) expert to search the records you will need and to give you many of the answers that will help you determine if the property is right for you. Title experts are equipped to handle most of the work discussed here, like last-owner searches, and they can direct you to other experts for answers to your questions.

Asking for the Terms of Sale before Bidding on Foreclosures at Auctions

In addition to asking your questions, if you plan on buying your foreclosure at an auction, I advise you to ask the foreclosing lender's attorney or the referee, sheriff, or trustee for an advance copy of the contract (also known as the Terms of Sale) that will be provided to the successful high bidder. This way, you can preview the contract terms and identify any stipulations that may cause problems, such as penalties for not closing, closing expenses that will be charged to the high bidder, and the like.

Uncovering Hidden Costs

When you are choosing the property that is right for you, you will need to know some of the hidden costs that you may not have been warned about on those late-night television infomercials. As is true for most real estate transactions, your actual expenses are more than just the purchase price of the property. Here are some additional costs that you should expect when you are considering a foreclosure purchase.

Insurance Policies

One of the additional expenses in the purchase of a property is the expense of insuring it. If you intend to live there, you will need a *homeowner's insurance policy* to protect your interests in the property as an owner-occupant.

If you intend to rent the property to tenants, you will need a *landlord's policy*, which provides a different type of coverage. Years ago, an investor told me about a rental property that he had just renovated at a cost of thousands of dollars. One week before the tenants were scheduled to move in, someone broke into the basement and completely destroyed the heating unit with a sledgehammer. The investor was not covered by his insurance. He would have been covered if the person who had broken into the house had removed the heating unit, because the investor had coverage for theft, but unfortunately, he didn't have vandalism insurance, and he was unable to recover the losses he had sustained. Landlords have special insurance needs that owner-occupants do not have. Choose an insurance provider who is experienced with landlord policies and who can explain the coverage that best protects your investment.

For investors who wish to rent out their property to others, a *rent-loss policy* is also recommended. In the event that a disaster, such as a fire, forces your tenant to vacate the premises, this rent-loss policy (like business interruption insurance) should insure you for lost rental income while your property is being repaired. Will this type of insurance cover you if a deadbeat tenant doesn't feel like paying the rent? Unfortunately, this policy is not for that type of rent loss. However, let's say you have a fire in a house that you rent out to others. You call the bank that lent you the money to buy the property, and you say, "Hello, XYZ Bank? We just had a fire in the house, and the tenants had to move out. We won't be receiving any rental income for a while, so we won't be able to pay our loan for a few months or so, okay?" What will XYZ Bank say? "See you at the foreclosure." This rent-loss insurance policy will cover the lost rental payments so that you can continue to pay your loan.

Another insurance expense is *title insurance*. In almost all real estate purchases, you will need to obtain title insurance to help protect you against title claims. Your attorney or title expert can help you choose the proper coverage.

If you are planning to rent out the house to others, it is best to qualify the prospective tenants and their ability to pay the rent each month. But what if the tenants have an accident and are unable to work? How are they going to pay the rent? Now you are stuck in the uncomfortable position of dealing with an injured tenant who can't pay you, as well as the possibility of a costly and lengthy eviction procedure. I suggest a *tenant's disability policy*, which provides coverage for tenants in the event that they become disabled and are unable to pay the rent. The cost of this type of policy will vary depending on the amount of coverage and the tenant's age, sex, and occupation; however, the cost can be as low as a few dollars a month. You can have your tenant buy the policy and name you (the landlord) as the beneficiary, or you can buy the policy for the tenant and be named as both the owner of the policy and the beneficiary. This may qualify for a tax deduction as a landlord's expense.

A *loan disability policy* is another type of insurance policy to consider when buying a foreclosure or any other type of real estate. What if you have an accident and are unable to work? Who will pay your loan? Will you be foreclosed on? Talk to your insurance expert or financial advisor to learn whether a disability policy that pays your home loan while you are disabled is beneficial for you.

Missing Property Documents

You may incur additional expenses if you must procure the missing documents discussed earlier in this chapter in order to purchase your foreclosure.

If you need to obtain a *survey*, the building department in the town (or city) in which the premises are located may already have this document on file. There is usually a minimal fee to obtain a copy. If the existing survey is more than 10 years old, or if there have been improvements to the premises that affect the structure and that do not appear on the original survey (such as a deck, an in-ground pool, a room extension or a new detached garage), you will need to have a new survey prepared.

This may be an expensive undertaking. Remember, if you are purchasing a property at an auction, you are purchasing that property in as-is condition, and there is no obligation for the referee, sheriff, or trustee to provide you with a new survey. On the other hand, if you are purchasing a property from a defaulting borrower or an REO from a bank or government agency, the terms of sale that you agree to in your contract will dictate whether or not the seller must pay the expenses involved and provide you with a survey and any other relevant property documents.

The *certificate of occupancy* (CO) or related proof of structural approval should also be on file with the town (or city) building department in the town (or city) where the premises are located. If a new CO is required, the normal procedure for obtaining one includes a visit from the local government (i.e., town, county, or village) inspector. The inspector will examine the premises to make sure that any additions or improvements were constructed in accordance with the local building codes. There may be additional violations that that will require costly repairs. These violations may not even have been applicable at the time that the structure was originally completed, but new, updated services may be required under current building codes. Once the proper permits are obtained, the local tax assessor may increase the property taxes to reflect the value that the improvements have added to the structure.

If you plan to rent the property out to others, you may need a *rental permit*. The permit procedure is often implemented by local government agencies, such as the town building department, to protect potential tenants from substandard living conditions. An inspection by the local building department and a fee for the permit may also be required.

Outstanding Utility Expenses

Additional utility expenses include water, electricity, and gas charges that may have accrued under the previous owner, or deposits that the utility company requires from new owners who wish to reinstate service. Cesspool certifications, well tests, and sewer hookups also fall into this category.

Repair Costs

This includes the costs of both structural and cosmetic repairs, in accordance with the reports given to you by your licensed contractor or engineer. Figure 9-4 is an example of an engineer's report. Going forward, in Chapter 13 we'll review how to hire and work with your contractor.

SAMPLE OF AN ENGINEER'S REPORT

I. OUTSIDE
1. GRADING: Good ☐ Fair ☐ Poor ☐ Low Spots: Yes___; 2. NO. ELECT. WIRES___Over☐ Under ☐ Capacity___Amps
3. TERMITES: None Apparent ☐ Evidences of ☐ : _____
4. EXTERIOR WALLS: Material _____
    Repairs Needed: Yes ☐ _____
5. ROOFING: Material: _____ Age: _____Years
    Repairs Needed: Yes ☐ _____
6. GUTTERS & LEADERS: Material_____ Drains/Drywells: Yes☐ No☐ ; Repair/Replacement:_____

II. SUPPORT STRUCTURE: MECHANICAL/ELECTRICAL
1. BSMT: Full ☐ Partial☐ CRAWL: ☐ SLAB: ☐ Full ☐ Partial ☐_____
2. WATER PENETRATION: Seepage ☐ Dampness ☐ _____
3. FLOOR: Concrete ☐ Wood ☐ Dirt ☐ ; Cracks: Some ☐ Many ☐ Texture: Smooth ☐ Rough ☐ Floor Drains: Yes☐
4. TERMITES: None Apparent ☐ Evidences of ☐ : _____
5. FOUNDATION WALLS: Material_____Condition_____Cracks: Yes ☐ No ☐ Not Visible ☐
6. COLUMNS: Material _____(Not) (Part) Visible ☐ Condition_____
7. GIRDERS: Material_____(Not) (Part) Visible ☐ Condition_____
8. FLOOR JOISTS: Size/Spacing/Span_____(Not) (Few) Visible ☐ Condition _____
9. HEATING SYSTEM: Hot Water☐ Hot Air☐ Steam ☐ ; Fuel: Gas☐ Oil☐ Elect.☐ ; No. of Zones_____Vented: Yes☐ No☐

III. ATTIC AREA
1. ROOF RAFTERS: Size & Spacing_____Standard ☐ Below Standard ☐ Evidences of Rot: Yes☐ No ☐
2. INSULATION: Floor ☐ Walls ☐ Roof ☐ None ☐ Vapor Barrier: Yes ☐ No ☐ Type and Thickness _____
3. FLOOR JOISTS: Size & Spacing:_____Can Accommodate Normal Storage: Yes ☐No ☐ Flooring: Yes ☐No☐ Partial☐
4. VENTILATION: Adequate ☐ More Needed ☐ None ☐ 5. LEAKS, Condensation: Yes ☐ No ☐_____

ROOM: _____
1. CEILING: Plaster ☐ Drywall ☐ Paneling ☐ Other ☐ _____ Cracks: Yes ☐ Leaks: Yes ☐ _____
2. WALLS: Plaster ☐ Drywall ☐ Paneling ☐ Tiles ☐ Other ☐ _____ Cracks: Yes ☐ Leaks: Yes ☐ _____
3. WINDOWS: No._____Type: Double Hung ☐ Casement ☐ Slider ☐ Jalousie ☐; Material: Wood ☐ Metal ☐ Vinyl ☐
    Wth'r. Stpd.: Yes ☐ No ☐ Cords Broken: Yes ☐ Insulated Glass ☐ Single Glass ☐ Storm: Yes ☐ No ☐
4. ELECTRIC OUTLETS: No._____ Wall Switches: Yes ☐ No ☐ Old ☐
5. FLOOR: Wood _____Tile ☐ Concrete ☐ Covered ☐ Condition: Acceptable ☐ Needs Repair ☐ Slopes ☐ Squeaks ☐
6. TRIM: Wood ☐ Tile☐ Steel ☐ Condition: Acceptable ☐ Needs Repair/Upgrading _____
7. HARDWARE: (Hinges, Locks, Knobs, etc.): Condition: Good ☐ Functional ☐ Old ☐ Need Repair☐
8. HEATING: Radiators_____Convectors _____Heat Grills _____ A/C Grill _____ Baseboard ☐ Radiant Htg. ☐ Pipe Riser ☐
9. DOORS: Exterior:_____ Good ☐ Acceptable ☐ Poor ☐ Repair/Replace _____
    Interior: _____ Good ☐ Acceptable ☐ Poor ☐ Repair/Replace _____
10. PLUMBING FIXTURES: Good ☐ Operating ☐ Replace _____Faucet Leaks: Yes ☐ _____Sink Drains_____
    Pressure: Normal ☐ Below Normal ☐ Tile Repairs Needed at Tub/Shower: Yes _____
11. APPLIANCES: STOVE: Gas ☐_____ Elect.☐_____REFRIGERATOR: None ☐ Operating ☐ Old ☐_____
    DISHWASHER: Functional ☐ Old ☐ Other_____

For more information, contact Taucher-Chronacker Professional Engineers (516) 766-1019
FOR ILLUSTRATION PURPOSES ONLY. REPRODUCTION PROHIBITED.

Figure 9-4. A sample engineer's report.

Eviction Costs

The burden of evicting the existing occupants from the premises may be on you, as the new owner, unless otherwise agreed. This will include court costs and legal fees, naturally, and if you are buying the foreclosure as an investor, don't forget to include the rent loss sustained during the eviction period.

Unpaid Property Taxes

The upset price of a property purchased at an auction usually includes the amount of the unpaid property taxes. However, you may be responsible for the property taxes that have accrued from the date of the auction until the day you close (approximately 30 days). This is because the property tax arrears can be figured accurately only for the period from the time the delinquency began until the date of the auction. Thus, if you have an expected closing period of 30 days between the auction date and the closing date, and property taxes are $5,000 per year, the costs can be calculated at $416. On the other hand, when you are purchasing an REO or a preforeclosure, your property tax responsibility generally begins on the day you become the new owner of the property.

Establishing Property Values

When you're choosing the property that is right for you, one of your primary concerns to avoid overpaying for your foreclosure will be establishing accurate property value. You will need to determine the market value of the property in a repaired condition, and there are several alternatives available to you.

You can look in your local newspapers for people who are selling properties that are similar in location and style to the foreclosure property you are interested in. Visit the advertised properties and compare them to the property that you have chosen to bid on. You will have to compare the sizes of the lots that the houses are built on, the number and sizes of the rooms, the properties' locations, the improvements that have been added, the property taxes, the school districts, and so on. This may help you get an idea of the value of the property you wish to bid on. However, this method is not very accurate because you will be basing your value on the asking prices of the people who are selling rather than on the prices that people have actually paid for properties, prices that would be significantly more accurate in the context of market value. This is especially true when the property was placed on the market nine months ago by an unmotivated seller at an inflated asking price "just to see if anyone is interested in buying it," and it has still not sold.

You can hire an appraiser to provide you with the value of the property (or properties) you are interested in. You will have an accurate report of market value, but appraisals can be expensive. If you are interested in 10 or 20 properties, then appraisal costs can quickly become prohibitive, especially since you have no guarantee that you will be the successful high bidder in an auction situation, and if you are going to submit an offer through any other method, you also have no guarantee that your offer will be accepted. Therefore, you may have wasted the money that you spent on the appraisals.

Another available alternative is both accurate and (in most cases) free. What if I took you up in my helicopter and dropped you (gently) in a strange town? How would you find out about where you landed? About the economic makeup of the area, where the stores and schools were, what the prices and values of houses were? Your best resource is your local real estate company. Most real estate professionals are experts on the neighborhoods they work in. For these reasons, I suggest that you contact two or three real estate offices that are in the immediate area of the property you are interested in. Ask them if they can provide a comparative market analysis (real estate jargon for an informal appraisal) to give you an accurate value of the property in a repaired condition. They will use their resources to determine the value of your property based on the selling prices of comparable properties in the immediate area that have been sold recently.

Calculating Cash Flow

If you are an investor who intends to use your foreclosure as a rental property or if you plan to purchase multiunit residential or commercial rental property, you will need to calculate your projected cash flow.

As briefly discussed in Chapter 8, cash flow is the money that flows into and out of a rental property. Normally, the rental income, less the repairs, carrying charges, and other operating expenses, determines the cash flow for a property. Different classifications of rental property require different methods of calculating cash flow. Cash flow calculations for small investment properties, such as one-, two-, or three-family houses, will be less complicated than those for larger multifamily or commercial properties. Your operating costs and expenses may include maintenance fees, management costs, and other costs that are part of the daily upkeep of larger properties. Contact your accountant or financial expert about cash flow projections if you intend to purchase foreclosures for investment purposes.

Figure 9-5 details an example of a cash flow projection for a single-family house in which the tenants are responsible for payment of all utilities and lawn-care services. In Figure 9-5, the monthly rental income must exceed the carrying charges of $1,716 in order to achieve a positive cash flow. A negative cash flow will result if the rental income is less than $1,716 a month. Repair expenses that exist at the time of the purchase have already been calculated as part of the cost of purchasing the property. The tenants will be paying for the monthly utilities; therefore, utilities are not included as part of the carrying charges.

You will need to verify carefully that your cash flow projections and monthly expenses are accurate. Any unrealistic cash flow expectations relating to monthly income and carrying charges can be disastrous. For example, in Figure 9-5, let's assume a projected monthly rental income of $1,800. This would yield an expected positive cash flow of $84 per month, since our carrying charges total $1,716. One of the monthly expenses is the real estate property taxes that you are expecting to pay. The present owner's taxes may be lower because of a tax exemption that you, as the new owner, are not eligible for. This includes senior citizen and veteran's property tax breaks. If you expected your property tax expense to be $416 per month because that's what the current

---

A Cash Flow Projection

Property: 123 Smith Street, Anytown, U.S.A.

Anticipated monthly rental income	$1,800
Monthly loan payment	$1,200
Monthly property taxes $5,000/yr	+ 416
Monthly property insurance	+ 100
Total carrying charges	$ 1,716
Monthly cash flow projection	$ + 84

($1,800 − $1,716 = $84)

Figure 9-5. An example of a cash flow projection for a single-family dwelling.

owner is paying, but the taxes are increased to $600 monthly when you become the new owner, your positive cash flow of $84 monthly becomes a negative cash flow of $100 monthly! Another property tax snag may come in the form of separately billed taxes, such as school taxes and incorporated village taxes, which are billed in addition to the property taxes. Also remember that (surprise, surprise!) there may be improvements for which the previous owner never obtained the proper (or any, for that matter) building permits, and once you have obtained these important documents, your property taxes may increase accordingly. If you have not considered all of these taxes, then the extra expense will cause a big problem for you from day one. As discussed earlier in this chapter, most property taxes can be verified at the tax assessor's office in the town (or city) where the premises are located.

Coming up in Chapter 10, we take the information we have gathered from our physical on-site inspections, the questions we asked, and the hidden expenses we uncovered, and we use it to formulate our bid sheets.

10

Preparing Your Bid Sheet

In Chapter 10, we implement the step-by-step procedures for calculating your expenses and preparing a bid sheet that you can use in determining the price that you will offer/bid for the foreclosure. This process helps you to organize your information, distinguish your foreclosure "wants" from your foreclosure "needs," redefine your priorities, and ultimately, avoid buying overpriced foreclosures.

If you have completed the preliminary research on several properties, Chapter 10 will also help you narrow down your selection of properties so that you can concentrate on those that are most worth pursuing.

Organizing Your Prebid Calculations

Follow these three steps as a basic guideline to organize your bid sheets: (1) estimate the market value of your foreclosure in a repaired condition, and if you are purchasing the foreclosure to use as a rental property, estimate the rental value as well; (2) estimate the projected expenses associated with purchasing and repairing the property; and (3) calculate your bid limits based on your personal financial situation and future goals.

Fine Tuning Your Prebid Calculations

In Chapter 9, we divided the condition of foreclosed properties into four categories to perform our preliminary research. Now, in Chapter 10, we revisit these four conditions—this time to fine tune our calculations for purchasing the properties we have selected.

Here are the steps to take for fine tuning your bid sheets for foreclosed properties in each of these four conditions:

- *Vacant and accessible:* no one lives there, and you can go inside and inspect.

- *Occupied and accessible:* someone lives there, and you can go inside and inspect.

- *Vacant and inaccessible:* no one lives there, and there is no access for you to go inside to inspect.

- *Occupied and inaccessible:* remember the angry, unfriendly occupant with the rabid pit bull and the loaded shotgun from Chapter 9?

Condition 1: Vacant and Accessible

Take the following steps to prepare bid sheets for properties that are vacant and accessible:

1. *Get prices for repairs.* Bring a licensed contractor and/or an engineer to the premises to uncover structural deficiencies and to give you a written, itemized estimate that includes the price of the repairs and the time it will take to complete them. As discussed in Chapter 9, make certain that the repairs can be completed in a time frame that complies with your insurance company's vacancy exclusion period limits.

2. *Determine the market value of the property in a repaired condition.* As explained in Chapter 9, you can estimate the value of a property by conducting your own research, by obtaining a professional appraisal, or by consulting with real estate professionals in the neighborhoods that are of interest to you. If you intend to rent the property out to tenants, you must also obtain estimates for rental income in order to prepare your cash flow analysis.

3. *Calculate your bid limits.* Generally, the market value of the property in a repaired condition, less the expenses and repairs required during and after the purchase, gives you a pretty accurate guideline for the price to pay for a break-even transaction. Once you have established the break-even point, you can make adjustments and prepare offers in accordance with your individual goals.

Figure 10-1 illustrates how the information you acquired during your preliminary preparations is applied to your bid sheet in order to calculate your bid limits accurately. Originally designed for the purpose of purchasing a foreclosure at an auction, this bid sheet may also be used for calculating offers to present to bank and government REO sellers and defaulting homeowners. In our example, the opening bid amount, or asking price, is $230,000. We have estimated the property's market value in a repaired condition to be $300,000. If the property is being purchased as an investment property to rent out to others, we will need to estimate the expected monthly rental income. In this case, the projected monthly rental income is $1,800.

BID-CALCULATING WORKSHEET

Opening bid amount	**$230,000**
Estimated market value repaired	**$300,000**
Anticipated monthly rental income	**$1,800**

Expenses

Estimated insurance	$1,000
Estimated loan	
Estimated loan cost	
Property document cost	
Utility expenses	
Repair costs	$10,000
Eviction costs	
Unpaid taxes	$400 ($5,000/year for 30 days, rounded off)
Anticipated rent loss	$1,800 (for 1 month during repairs)
Other expenses	
Total expenses	$13,200
Estimated market value	**$300,000**
Deduct expenses	**−($13,200)**
Amount to bid for a break-even purchase	**$286,800**

Figure 10-1. A bid-calculating worksheet.

Next, we estimate our expenses, those that will be incurred before, during, and after the closing. The expenses that are incurred before and at the time of the closing are usually those that are associated with the purchase itself (i.e., insurance policies, loan financing, closing costs, property documents, utility expenses, unpaid taxes, appraisals, engineer reports, and other such costs). Also please note that in some states the purchaser pays the state transfer taxes on property purchased at a bank foreclosure auction. Expenses that are usually incurred after the closing include repair costs, eviction expenses, and the cost of rent loss. In Figure 10-1, we have estimated our insurance costs (including title insurance and property insurance) to be $1,000. There are no loan financing costs included because we are purchasing the property with cash; therefore, no loan is needed. We have estimated our repair expenses to be $10,000, based on estimates from our contractor and our engineer. Our contractor estimated that it would take one month to complete the repairs; therefore, we must include a rent-loss expense of $1,800 in our calculations. We have confirmed that the unpaid property taxes total $400 (rounded off) for the 30 days between the contract and the closing, based on the property tax amount of $5,000 a year. Our total expenses add up to $13,200.

We have estimated the market value of the property in a repaired condition to be $300,000. From this number, we deduct $13,200 for expenses, which gives us our amount to bid for a "breakeven purchase price" of $286,800. If the auction contract terms require a 10 percent down payment from the successful high bidder, we would bring $28,600 with us to the auction. Right? Good.

But wait a moment . . . did we just say that we are buying a property for $286,800 and spending another $13,200 on repairs, and the property is going to be worth only $300,000? Why don't we just buy a traditional resale for $300,000 and save ourselves a lot of extra work?

Well, $286,800 is just the breakeven price—the price we would offer if we expected to pay full market price (i.e., if we paid one dollar on the dollar). Once we have established the breakeven price, we can adjust our offers according to our goals. For example, someone who wants to buy the house to live in and raise a family may be better off paying 90 cents on the dollar (90 percent of value) up to one dollar on the dollar (100 percent of value) now and waiting to collect a profit after the property is sold, in years to come. For this buyer, the primary goal is a long-term home. By contrast, the primary goal for investors and profit-oriented buyers is a discounted purchase price. On average, these kinds of buyers limit their purchases to 75 percent of our $300,000 (i.e., 75 cents on the dollar), or $225,000 as a starting point, from which we deduct our $13,200 expenses. So, in our example, we end up with a maximum bid limit of $211,800. Since the opening bid amount in our example starts at $230,000 at the auction, this property would not be attractive to us as investors unless the referee, sheriff, or trustee can accept less than the opening bid amount at the auction.

Sometimes a buyer at an auction bids much higher than we would have. It is possible that the buyer has either overestimated the property value or underestimated the expenses. On the other hand, the buyer may be a contractor and already have the materials needed (which in our example would have cost us $10,000) stored in his or her garage. If that is the case, that contractor can bid higher—and has a better chance of getting the property—than someone who does not have the same advantage. The same thing may hold true in a situation where there are anticipated legal fees and the bidder is a real estate attorney who will get the benefit of lower legal fees than the next bidder.

The process of preparing your bid sheet not only helps you calculate your final bidding price but also prevents you from being caught up in "auction fever"—a situation where the competitive atmosphere overcomes your common sense and you keep bidding even after the price exceeds the property value. How does your bid sheet prevent this craziness? Because you bring only enough money with you to cover the required down payment—10 percent of your bid sheet calculations—so the maximum amount you can bid is limited to the price limit you set for yourself when you were sane.

You can use this same bid-calculating worksheet to prepare your written offers for REO properties and to purchase homes from defaulting borrowers. Financing fees and loan expenses can vary significantly from state to state, and you should consult with experts in your state (i.e., your loan officer, your attorney, your financial advisor, your accountant, your lender, and other such people) to make sure that you have taken all of your expenses into consideration.

Condition 2: Occupied and Accessible

In this situation, the occupants allow you to enter the property. You will therefore have an opportunity to view the property and meet the occupants. Take the following steps to prepare bid sheets for properties that are occupied and accessible:

1. *Obtain estimates for repairs.* Bring your contractor or engineer and get reports and estimates of repairs for your bid sheet calculations, including the length of time for completion. You can also ask the

occupants about any structural or appliance defects or problems that the occupants are having with the plumbing, heating, and electrical systems and include the costs for any repairs that are needed as well.

2. *Inquire about the present occupants' preference regarding continued occupancy.* The occupants are either the defaulting borrowers or their tenants. Sometimes the tenants are in shock when you show up to inspect the property. They have been paying their rent each month, and they had no idea that the landlord was not repaying the loan. Sometimes, however, it is the tenants who are causing the foreclosure—by not paying their rent.

If the occupants are tenants of the defaulting owners and you intend to rent out the property if you are the successful bidder, you may want to offer the tenants a new lease with you. Most state laws provide that, as long as there was proper service of the legal documents when the foreclosure action began, you, as the new owner, are not bound by the present tenant's previous lease with the defaulting borrower, because leases are subordinate to home loans. Ask your attorney whether this is the case in your state. You are also not responsible for refunding any security deposits that the tenants may have given the previous owner, and the tenants should be made aware that they must look to the previous owner for reimbursement of the deposits.

If you expect to live in the property yourself and wish to have the occupants evicted or if the occupants seem undesirable (one hint may be if there are five cars disassembled into piles of rusting debris on the front lawn) and you want them to leave, you can add eviction expenses to your bid calculations.

If the occupants were the previous owners, you may wish to negotiate rental terms with them should you become the new owner. If such terms can be negotiated, you would allow them to stay in the property under the terms of a new lease with you. One property I inspected was occupied by the defaulting owners who were being foreclosed on. They had kept the place in excellent condition, and they wanted to know if I would let them stay if I were the successful bidder. Their son was about to begin his last year in high school, and they didn't want to move until after his graduation. They had been very helpful and accommodating, and they let me inspect the property several times. These people were good potential tenants. They had kept the place clean and in good condition, they were highly motivated to continue to live there as tenants, and they would be very conscientious about paying their rent on time in order to remain there. Also, the fact that someone is being foreclosed on does not always eliminate that person as a candidate for renting the property. While it may be true that the person could not afford the $1,200 home loan and the $1,500 junior lien on the property when he or she was the owner, that person can very possibly afford the $1,800 per month that you would be charging for rent. A word of caution here: please contact your attorney or local real estate expert in order to ascertain whether your state has adopted a Home Equity Theft Protection Act (discussed in Chapter 5) that prohibits agreements allowing defaulting homeowners to remain in occupancy after the closing of title. This Act generally focuses on agreements with the defaulting homeowner but it does not always prohibit an agreement with the tenants of the defaulting homeowner that allows them to stay under a new lease with you.

3. *Calculate your bid limits.* Prepare your bid sheet in the same manner as when the property was vacant but accessible; however, if there is an anticipated eviction looming on the horizon, that cost must be added to your expenses. Also remember to include the cost of lost rent that may be incurred during the eviction proceedings. Contact an attorney with experience in performing legal evictions for a more accurate estimate of these costs.

Condition 3: Vacant and Inaccessible

This is the least desirable condition in foreclosure bidding. In this situation, you are bidding on a property that you are unable to inspect. Sometimes access to the property is denied as an administrative requirement by the insurance policy carrier, and sometimes access is denied because the house has so much structural damage (e.g., floors or ceilings that are caving in) that it would be dangerous to allow people in to inspect it.

You could be bidding on a property that is a complete disaster. Even if the property looks okay on the outside, there is absolutely no guarantee that the inside is in good condition. I have encountered collapsed cesspools, polluted wells, sewer hookups that are only partially completed, broken pipes, frozen pipes, and no pipes. It almost seemed as though the people who were foreclosed on said to themselves, "If I can't have this house, then neither can anyone else!"

Your repair costs may equal or exceed the purchase price. This is not a recommended situation for someone who is new at purchasing foreclosures. Preparing a bid sheet is difficult when you cannot determine your repair expenses, and a mistaken "guesstimate" can cost thousands of dollars.

In addition, most lenders will not finance a home loan if the bank appraiser is unable to get access to the inside of the premises to check that the plumbing, heating, and electrical systems are in good working order and to see if there are major structural repairs that need to be completed. Buying a property that you cannot inspect first is like buying a car without looking under the hood. Unless you are very handy and can afford to make repairs at minimal costs, or you plan to knock the structure down completely and rebuild from scratch, avoid foreclosures that are vacant and inaccessible. Move on and look for a different property where you can get inside to inspect.

Condition 4: Occupied and Inaccessible

Properties that are occupied but inaccessible are also very risky. You may be encountering bitter, unfriendly people who refuse to cooperate and won't allow you into the house to inspect it before you bid. In such situations, I have been able to gain access to the house by sympathizing with the people who reside there. Sometimes, if the occupants appeared to be taking good care of the property and I intended to rent the property to tenants anyway, I offered them the opportunity to remain there under a new lease with me if I was the high bidder. As a reminder, please contact your attorney or local real estate expert to ascertain whether your state has adopted a Home Equity Theft Prevention Act that prohibits allowing the defaulting borrower to remain in occupancy after the closing of title. Again, this Act generally does not prohibit agreements with the tenants allowing them to stay beyond the closing date.

Negotiating vacancy agreements.   In the event that you wish to move into the property yourself or if you do not wish to offer the current occupants a lease for any reason, I have found it very effective to offer moving money (dollar compensation, also known as "cash for keys") to pay the costs of moving expenses for the occupants. This amount is added to your bid calculations as another expense. Do we just whip out our wallets and pay them? Of course not! We haven't even gone to the auction yet. We sign an agreement that if we are the successful high bidders, we will pay the occupants a preagreed amount after we own the property, after they have removed all of their belongings, and if the premises are left in broom-clean and good condition. Money is given to the occupants only after they have fulfilled their end of the agreement, moved out, and turned the keys over to you. Money is a very effective tool to offer to offset the inconvenience of moving and as an incentive for potentially hostile occupants to leave both quickly and peacefully.

BEFORE YOU BID DO THE FOLLOWING

☐ Determine the "purchase price" range that best reflects your current financial situation and your future goals.

☐ Ask the "prebid" questions.

☐ Inspect the premises.

☐ Research the status of missing documents (i.e., survey, Certificate of Occupancy, and so on).

☐ Get a written estimate for repairs from a licensed contractor and/or engineer.

☐ Inspect the file of the foreclosure action (if possible).

☐ Determine the market value of the property in a repaired condition.

☐ Determine the rental value, if applicable.

☐ Calculate expenses.

☐ Consider the status of current occupants (if applicable).

☐ Research eviction fees and the time for completion (if necessary).

☐ Calculate your bid limits on a bid sheet.

☐ Contact the referee, sheriff, or trustee or the foreclosing lender's attorney to confirm the final upset price.

☐ Contact the referee, sheriff, or trustee or the foreclosing lender's attorney to confirm that the auction is still on.

Please note: Not all-inclusive—additional information may be required.

Figure 10-2. A sample checklist: prior to bidding.

At any rate, extreme caution is urged if you wish to buy a foreclosure under these circumstances. The potential risks are obvious, and the purchase may be costly because you will be dealing with unfriendly occupants who are in a position to cause significant damage to the property. It may not be worth the time or money you would be expending.

Final Confirmation

Two final preliminary preparations are suggested. The first concerns bidding at an auction; the second concerns mailing in a written offer for a bank or government REO or a preforeclosure.

Before bidding on a foreclosure at an auction, you should contact the referee, sheriff, or trustee or designated authority to confirm that the sale is still on, and that the defaulting borrowers have not filed for bankruptcy and stopped the foreclosure, obtained an extension of their existing loan, or exercised their right of redemption by paying all the arrears. Also confirm the final opening bid amount. Sometimes the opening bid will be higher than the amount that was originally published because of additional legal fees or other expenses.

Last, in the event that you are submitting your bid to purchase a foreclosure through a written offer, be sure to follow up on the status of your offer daily until you know whether it has been accepted or rejected.

An example of a checklist for use prior to bidding is included as Figure 10-2. The checklist combines the preliminary research preparations from Chapter 9 with the preliminary bid sheet preparations from Chapter 10. The checklist is not all-inclusive, and you should customize and supplement the list with additional tasks that you must complete in accordance with your specific purchasing strategy.

11

Congratulations! You Are the Successful High Bidder

Once your offer or bid has been accepted, you can hit the ground running if you have a plan of action and procedures in place to help you complete the transaction.

In Chapter 11, we review the procedures to follow for purchasing foreclosures when (1) you are the high bidder at an auction, (2) your offer for a bank-owned or government-owned REO property has been accepted by the seller, or (3) you have successfully negotiated the price and terms for a preauction foreclosure with the defaulting borrower.

When You Are the High Bidder at the Auction

When you are the successful high bidder at an auction and you are awarded the sales contract, your first priority is to prepare yourself for the final closing arrangements. This is because time is usually of the essence—many foreclosure auctions require a 30-day closing, which leaves you with a lot to accomplish in an abbreviated time frame. The paperwork you receive from the referee, sheriff, or trustee should document the terms of the sale, including the date on which you are expected to close, the amount of your down payment, and the remaining balance due at closing. Verify the answers to all of your prebid questions, including repair responsibility and costs, insurance requirements, occupancy status, and the availability of property documents (i.e., certificate of occupancy, survey, and so on). If you have not already done so, you should contact your attorney, your loan officer, your financial advisor, and any other professionals who will be assisting you in completing your purchase. *If you are purchasing the foreclosure with cash,* confirm the final amount that you will need for your closing costs. *If you are financing the foreclosure with a loan from a lending institution* (and, hopefully, have already obtained a preapproval from the lender you will be borrowing from), contact your attorney, your loan officer, and/or financial advisor to ask about the next steps to take to prepare for the closing, now that you have your contract from the referee, sheriff, or trustee.

When Your Offer for a Bank- or Government-Owned REO Foreclosure Is Accepted

After your offer has been accepted by a bank or a government agency and the contract documents are issued, your attorney, your loan officer, should examine the terms of the sale and explain the rest of the process to you so that you know what to expect. *If you are buying the foreclosure with cash*, confirm the accuracy of your closing cost calculations with your attorney, your loan officer, and/or your financial advisor. *If the bank or government agency that accepted your offer is also providing the financing for the foreclosure*, or *if you are financing the foreclosure with a loan from a different lending institution*, your attorney should verify and explain the terms, conditions, and closing costs.

When Your Offer to the Defaulting Borrower for a Preforeclosure Is Accepted

After the defaulting borrower accepts your offer, arrange to get your agreement in writing. Depending on the custom in your area, one of the parties (or his or her attorney) will prepare a sales contract that sets forth the terms and conditions that you and the seller have agreed to. If the defaulting borrower provides the contract, review it carefully to ensure that the terms stipulated in the contract are in accordance with your expectations, based on the agreement that you made with the seller. Your attorney will order a title report to ensure that there are no additional liens or judgments. Your attorney should also verify any financing terms that you arranged with the foreclosing lender. For example, if you arranged to assume the defaulting borrower's outstanding loan balance, your attorney should finalize the assumption terms. If you will be obtaining financing from another source, your attorney and the lending institution's loan officer should assist in preparing you for the closing.

Unlike auctions and bank or government foreclosure sales, where you are purchasing the premises in an as-is condition, you have more negotiating power when it comes to the sales terms in a preauction purchase because you are negotiating directly with the owners, who are in control of the personal and real property that they are selling you. For example, your contract negotiations should address the specific fixtures and appliances that are included in the sale, and should describe them in detail. (Taking photos and preparing a fixtures and appliance list that can be added as a rider to the sales contract is also highly recommended.) Does the sale include the air conditioner that was installed in the living room wall? How about the one in the master bedroom window? Which refrigerator is staying with the house: the new frost-free model with the external ice water/ice cube dispenser, or the 1960 model stored in the basement? Don't forget landscaping; will the seller be leaving all of the shrubs, trees, and plants? Are the expensive window treatments and decorative doorknobs included in the sale? The closing date, lead paint disclosures, and property condition disclosures (if applicable), lease terms (if tenants are currently occupying the premises), vacating terms (for occupants to move out), security refunds (if applicable), and other such information should also be included as part of the contract agreement.

Coast to the Closing with These Five Standard Operating Procedures

These standard operating procedures can help you organize your priorities and eliminate closing delays.

Standard Operating Procedure 1: Order Your Appropriate Insurance

If you will be living in the premises, you will need a homeowner's insurance policy (for an owner-occupied dwelling). If you will be renting the property out to tenants, you will need a landlord's policy (for a non-owner-occupied dwelling). Remember to ensure that your coverage complies with the insurance company's vacancy exclusion period. Also, you may need a special flood policy if your foreclosure is located close to water. Contact your insurance agent to discuss the best rates and terms for your individual needs.

Standard Operating Procedure 2: Protect the Premises

If the property is vacant, confirm that it has been secured in a manner that prevents trespasser intrusion and vandalism. Most insurance companies will either arrange to have vacant houses boarded up by their own contractors or provide the owner with the requisite board-up specifications, which the owner can pass along to his or her own contractors. If the foreclosing lender is responsible for the care and protection of the premises until the closing, you should document the condition of the property immediately, including signed and dated pictures, videotapes, and witnesses.

As an example, if there were 12 unbroken windows in the house when you were the high bidder, then there should be 12 unbroken windows when you close on the property. If the property was boarded up, doors and windows were most likely removed first. You should request information about the location of those windows and doors. The foreclosing lender's insurance should cover any damages. Another option is to have an alarm system installed that is monitored 24 hours a day, 7 days a week by a central station operator who can ensure that the police (and you) are notified if the alarm is activated.

If the property is occupied, your contract with the lending institution probably stipulates that (aside from casualty such as fire or smoke damage) it will not be responsible for any cosmetic damages to the premises caused by the occupants. In most cases, any repairs that will be needed after you close will be your responsibility in this situation.

Standard Operating Procedure 3: Hire a Neighbor

Visit the next-door neighbors and express your concern for the safety of your new purchase. Since you will be making improvements to what may be considered the neighborhood "eyesore," the neighbors are likely to be extremely cooperative. Try to find that omnipresent, ever-watchful neighbor who knows at every moment exactly what's going on in every house in the neighborhood. Pay him or her to put this natural talent to good use. Offer a fee for house-watching services that simply involve notifying you, or the police, of any break-ins or other disturbances. Provide a contact number so that this person can reach you in case there are problems.

To protect houses that are vacant, some people can be quite creative. One investor told me about a technique he used to discourage break-ins: if one of his properties was vacant, he posted a sign with a skull and crossbones on the front door that read, "Danger! Poison Gas Leak" in large letters. No one ever broke into his houses! This example was just for illustration purposes, to show the extremes that some people with go to when protecting a vacant house, and *is not* recommended as a remedy—your neighbors are likely to freak out if they walk out their front doors and see a poison gas warning posted on a house that is just 20 feet away!

Standard Operating Procedure 4:
Order a Title Search and
Title Insurance

Under no circumstances should you take a chance on closing without first obtaining the title report and title insurance. The purpose of ordering the title report and title insurance is to help you uncover any existing liens or judgments that are currently attached to the property. While in most cases, property that is bank-owned or owned by a government agency will be sold free and clear of any other encumbrances, there is no guarantee to that effect. The title report is particularly valuable for a preauction purchaser because it can uncover that third junior lien on the property that the defaulting borrower "forgot" to disclose to you, and that you as the new owner could have been responsible for.

The title report will also reveal private land-use restrictions or encumbrances that could make the property difficult or impossible to sell in the future.

One other option that many purchasers find especially valuable is to have the title company "insure the survey" in order to verify that it is an accurate illustration of the property's legal description and dimensions.

Standard Operating Procedure 5:
Apply for Your Financing
(if Applicable)

If you have purchased a property at an auction that requires a specific closing date (such as 30 days), or if you have signed a contract with a "time is of the essence" closing date that is within 30 or even 60 days, hopefully you have expedited the financing procedure by getting preapproved for a mortgage loan before you bid on any properties. (See "Prequalified versus Preapproved" in Chapter 6.) During the loan processing procedure, you can further expedite the loan approval by providing bank personnel or appraisers with access to inspect the property as quickly as possible. Remember, financing may be delayed if the premises are occupied by unfriendly occupants who won't allow the lending institution's representatives inside to perform their inspections. Delays may also occur if the structure or systems need major repairs. The risk here is that if you are unable to obtain your financing by your deadline, you could lose your down payment—unless, of course, you can come up with the balance of your purchase price in cash. You may have to secure interim financing in order to close. Have your attorney review your sales contract with you to ensure that you understand all the conditions that you are expected to comply with.

In cases where the REO seller is providing you with financing for the property that you are purchasing from its inventory, closing rules may vary from one REO seller to the next. Your attorney can help advise you about the specific financing conditions that apply in your situation.

If you have purchased your foreclosure from a government agency (HUD, DVA, GSA, FDIC, or some other agency), and the agency is also providing you with financing, you should confirm the financing and closing procedures. Have your attorney review your paperwork so that you are familiar with your specific role and responsibilities. Again, your cooperation in responding to any requests for additional information from the lender will expedite the loan approval process significantly.

Applying the Five Standard Operating Procedures to Your Particular Circumstances

Once your offer has been accepted and your sales contract is executed, you can apply the standard operating procedures to each of the four property conditions that were enumerated in Chapter 9 in the context of preliminary research preparation, and in Chapter 10 in the context of bid sheet preparations. In Chapter 11, we revisit the four conditions once again—this time in the context of "after-contract preparations." Let's go through these procedures now in a step-by-step fashion.

After Contract: Implementing the Standard Operating Procedures for Vacant and Accessible Foreclosures

1. *Follow the five standard operating procedures set forth earlier in this chapter.*

2. *Get your rental permit.* If you intend to rent the property to tenants, and a rental permit is required, contact the building department, or other appropriate agency, and begin the procedure to obtain this document.

3. *Market the property.* If you intend to market the property for sale or rent, and the repairs needed are negligible, begin your advertising now. Once a tenant has been found, a lease or rental agreement can be negotiated and prepared for signature. Be sensitive to the fact that once you close, you are losing money every day that the premises are vacant. Therefore, if the tenant can take possession on the day you close, this will ensure that you receive immediate rental income.

After Contract: Implementing the Standard Operating Procedures for Occupied and Accessible Foreclosures

1. *Follow the five standard operating procedures set forth earlier in this chapter.*

2. *Contact the occupants.* Send what I call a "greetings" letter by both certified and first-class mail. The first-class letter is sent as a courtesy; that is, if the occupants are unable to go to the post office to pick up the certified letter, they will still receive your notification via first-class mail. The occupants whom you are addressing in this letter were cooperative and allowed you to inspect the property before you bid on it or made your offer to purchase it. When the occupants receive your letter and contact you, any agreements that you made during your previous inspections can now be finalized. As a reminder, please contact your attorney or local real estate expert to ascertain whether your state has adopted a Home Equity Theft Protection Act (discussed in Chapter 5) that prohibits any agreement allowing defaulting borrowers to remain in occupancy after the closing of title.

   Figure 11-1 is a sample greetings letter sent to cooperative occupants. Use this letter when

   - You have acquired the property at an auction and the property is occupied by either the defaulting borrowers or their tenant(s).

   - You purchased the property as a result of negotiations with the defaulting borrowers, and the occupants are their tenant(s).

   - The property is an REO, and the occupants are either the previous homeowners who were foreclosed on or their tenant(s).

   - You have purchased the property from a government agency, and the occupants are the previous homeowners or their tenant(s).

3. *If the occupants will be renting the premises from you,* you can have a lease or rental agreement prepared and ready to sign on the day you close. Let the occupants preview the lease so that any problems can be resolved in advance. Remind them (if applicable) that they must look to their previous landlord for any security deposit refunds that are due them under their old lease, and provide them with the details about the security deposit they will need when they sign the new lease with you.

4. *If the occupants will be moving out,* you should organize this arrangement so that you are aware of, and therefore in better control of, the

GREETINGS LETTER—SENT TO COOPERATIVE OCCUPANTS

(Send via certified mail, return receipt requested, and first class)

Today's date:

Dear _____ :
        (Occupant's name)

This is to advise you that I have purchased the property that you are occupying (at an auction I attended)/(from the bank)/(from the government agency) on _____ .
                          (Date of auction/Contract
                               with REO seller)

Please contact the undersigned at your earliest convenience to discuss this matter further.

My telephone number is (   ) _____ .
                          (Area code and telephone number)

The best time to reach me is _____ .
                               (Day and time)

Very truly yours,

_____
(Your signature)

Figure 11-1. An example of a greetings letter to cooperative occupants.

vacating procedure. You will need to know the date on which the occupants will be moving out so that you can arrange to be there to collect the keys and to secure the premises.

After Contract: Implementing the Standard Operating Procedures for Vacant and Inaccessible Foreclosures

1. *Follow the five standard operating procedures set forth earlier in this chapter.*

2. *Continue to inspect the premises on a regular basis.* If vandalism occurs, inform the designated authority so that proper insurance procedures can be followed.

3. *If you have taken possession of the property and are responsible for any damages*, you will need to advise your own insurance agency of any claims.

After Contract: Implementing the Standard Operating Procedures for Occupied and Inaccessible Foreclosures

1. *Follow the five standard operating procedures set forth earlier in this chapter.*

2. *Contact the occupants.* Send a greetings letter to the occupants. Unlike the greetings letter sent to the cooperative occupants, this letter is being sent to occupants who did not cooperate with you during your initial attempt to gain access to the premises. Any response you receive from these occupants will help determine your next move— eviction, a new lease, or moving money. Use the same mailing protocol for uncooperative occupants as for cooperative occupants (i.e., send the greetings letter both certified and first class). Once again, ascertain whether your state has adopted a Home Equity Theft Protection Act (discussed in Chapter 5) that prohibits any agreement allowing defaulting borrowers to remain in occupancy after the closing of title.

Figure 11-2 is a sample greetings letter to uncooperative occupants. Use this letter when

- Your attempts to contact the occupants have been unsuccessful.

- The occupants have not responded to previous requests that they contact you, and you will be initiating legal eviction procedures to get them out. If the eviction laws in your state require tenant notification

GREETINGS LETTER—SENT TO UNCOOPERATIVE OCCUPANTS

(Send via certified mail, return receipt requested, and first class)

Today's date:

Dear _____:
       (Occupant's name)

This is to advise you that I have purchased the property that you are occupying (at an auction I attended)/(from the bank)/(from the government agency) on _____.
                (Date of auction/Contract
                 with REO seller)

I have been advised that you are still occupying the property, and I would appreciate it if you could contact me concerning your plans to move out. I understand the inconvenience that this may cause, and I would like to discuss financial assistance that I may be able to offer you toward moving costs or other expenses.

Please contact the undersigned at your earliest convenience to discuss this matter further.

My telephone number is (   ) _____.
                (Area code and telephone number)

The best time to reach me is _____.
                (Day and time)

Very truly yours,

_____
      (Your signature)

Figure 11-2. An example of a greetings letter to uncooperative occupants.

prior to initiating an eviction proceeding, you can produce the certified letter that was returned to you undelivered by the post office as evidence that you attempted to communicate with the occupants.

- You want to get the occupants' attention by offering moving money in return for their cooperation.

3. *If the occupants ask about renting the premises from you,* and you want to consider them as potential tenants, you can have a lease or rental agreement prepared and ready to sign on the day you close. Just as with the cooperative occupants, let the occupants preview the lease so that any problems can be resolved and questions answered in advance. Remind them (if applicable) that they must look to their previous landlord for any security deposit refunds that are due them under their old lease, and provide them with the details about the security deposit that they will need when they sign a new lease with you. Once again, ascertain whether your state has adopted a Home Equity Theft Protection Act (discussed in Chapter 5) that prohibits any agreement allowing defaulting borrowers to remain in occupancy after the closing of title.

4. *If the occupants will be moving out,* you should organize this arrangement so that you are aware of, and therefore in control of, the vacating procedure. You will have to draw up an agreement with the terms that you have agreed to, including the amount of money you will pay and the conditions that the occupants must meet in return for the payment.

An After-Contract Checklist

Figure 11-3 is a basic checklist of things to be done after the contract has been signed. This checklist is not intended to be all-inclusive, and you should customize and supplement the list with additional tasks that you must complete in accordance with your specific purchasing strategy.

<u>AFTER THE CONTRACT IS SIGNED, DO THE FOLLOWING:</u>

❏   Order the appropriate property insurance.

❏   Take pictures of the property to preserve a record of its condition.

❏   Protect the premises.

❏   Hire a neighbor.

❏   Order a title search and title insurance.

❏   Apply for financing (if applicable).

❏   Obtain a rental permit (if required).

❏   Market the property (if desired).

❏   Ascertain compliance with any Home Equity Theft Protection Act adopted in your state.

❏   Send out greetings letters (if necessary).

❏   Organize vacancy arrangements with occupants (if applicable).

Please note—Not all-inclusive—additional information may be required

---

Figure 11-3.   A sample checklist: after the contract.

12

Now that You Own the Property

After you close on your foreclosure and are the proud new owner of the property, you still have a few more steps to take. So, pat yourself on the back and follow along to complete the transaction.

Steps to Take for Completing the Transaction

Record the Closing Documents

Your attorney should make certain that your closing documents are properly recorded. If you are not represented by an attorney, ensure that the person who customarily is charged with bringing the applicable documents (deed, financing documents, and so on) to the recording office is providing this service for you.

Schedule the Repair Work

If you will be completing the repair work yourself or you are hiring a licensed contractor, you can begin the repairs on your foreclosure after you close. If you are planning to rent the property out to tenants and the property is vacant now, it is important that repairs be made as expeditiously as possible in order to avoid costly rental income losses. (Chapter 13 covers procedures for making repairs to your foreclosure.)

Restore the Utility Services

If your foreclosure is currently vacant and in need of repairs, the utilities (water, gas, and electricity) should be turned on so that work can begin quickly.

If the utilities are in the previous owner's name, as in an REO or government foreclosure purchase, have them transferred to your name to avoid service interruptions. If you have tenants moving in and your rental agreement stipulates that they will be responsible for utility services, advise them to contact the utility companies to have service transferred to their names before they move in. (The utility companies may require a deposit from your tenants if they are new customers.)

Begin Eviction Proceedings (if Applicable)

Depending on the legal requirements in your state, the eviction of any occupants living in the premises may be delayed until the deed has been recorded in the town or county clerk's office. If there is a recording backlog and the deed cannot be recorded for a long period of time, this could delay the eviction procedure. You should consult your attorney for the proper procedure to follow. The recording office personnel may also be able to give you some suggestions on how to expedite this procedure.

Contact Your Local Tax Collector

Contact the tax collector's office in the town in which your new property is located and let the office know of your new ownership. If you have obtained or assumed financing that requires an escrow for property taxes, the lender will collect the taxes as part of your monthly loan payment and will be responsible for forwarding payments directly to the tax collector in a timely manner. On the other hand, if you have purchased your foreclosure with cash, or if the lender does not escrow for real estate property taxes, you will be responsible for payment of the property taxes directly to the tax collector.

Once the deed showing you as the new owner is recorded, the tax collector will have notice of your new ownership and can forward the new tax bills to you. If, however, there is a backlog in the recording office, there may be delays in sending you the new tax bills. This could result in your being charged penalties for late payments.

To help prevent unnecessary delays with your property tax bill, send a letter to the tax collector's office identifying yourself as the new owner. Include the property description of your foreclosure to help the tax collector identify your property correctly. Send the letter by certified mail, and request that all future tax bills be sent to you at the appropriate address for payment. In the event that late charges or penalties accrue because of the tax collector's failure to send you the new tax bills, you may be able to have the penalties abated as long as

---

AFTER THE CLOSING, DO THE FOLLOWING:

( ) Closing documents should be recorded, as required.

( ) Begin necessary repair work.

( ) Restore utility services.

( ) Begin eviction proceedings (if required).

( ) Advise the tax collector(s) of your new ownership.

( ) Execute the lease with your tenants (if applicable).

Not all-inclusive—additional information may be required

Figure 12-1. A sample checklist: after the closing.

you can prove that you notified tax collecting authorities of the local school district, town, village, county, or other entity (preferably via a certified letter) of your new ownership.

Execute the Lease

If you have arranged for tenants to rent the property, you can now execute the lease or rental agreement with them. It is helpful to review all the terms of the lease or rental agreement with your tenants. Make certain that the tenants are aware of the date the rent is due and where it should be sent each month. Confirm the move-in date and the amount of the security deposit you will be collecting. If the tenants are already occupying the property because they were the tenants of the previous owners or if the previous owners are going to remain there as your tenants under new lease terms with you, then a new lease agreement should be executed and a new security deposit collected. Ascertain whether your state has adopted a Home Equity Theft Protection Act (discussed in Chapter 5) that prohibits any agreement allowing defaulting borrowers to remain in occupancy after the closing of title.

An After-Closing Checklist

Figure 12-1 is a basic checklist of things to be done after the closing has taken place. It is not intended to be all-inclusive, and you should customize and supplement the list with additional tasks that you must complete in accordance with your specific purchasing strategy.

13

Making Repairs to Your Foreclosure

Foreclosures are indicative of a distressed situation. People who are experiencing financial difficulties cannot afford to keep their property in prime condition. Therefore, the foreclosure you purchase may require extensive structural and/or cosmetic repairs. If you are the kind of person who thinks that a "square" is a skinny guy with glasses who prefers reading books to playing sports, and that a "wood plane" is something people utilized to navigate the skies in the early 1900s, then do not attempt to do your own repairs. Instead, you should consider hiring a contractor to work on your foreclosure.

In Chapter 13, we combine a "competitive bidding system" with a "payment for performance initiative" so that your repairs to your foreclosure can be completed in a timely and cost-effective manner.

Pinpointing Priorities

During the years that I worked as a residential property manager, one of my responsibilities was to hire contractors to repair and/or renovate investment properties. To accomplish this task with efficiency and cost-effectiveness, I implemented a procedure that combined a "competitive bidding system" with a "payment for performance initiative." This procedure was successful because it satisfied the needs of both parties: the property owners, whose priorities were (1) to have a professional quality of work completed (2) for a fair price and (3) in a timely fashion, and the contractors, who wanted (1) to perform work that was clearly defined in a formal agreement and (2) to be paid for completing that work on a steady basis as the work progressed.

Finding a Contractor

If you hired an engineer to give you a report on the property before you purchased it, he or she may be able to recommend a contractor. Or you can ask friends, coworkers, and neighbors who have recently had work done on their homes that is similar to the work you are planning to recommend a contractor that they were happy with. Another way to find a contractor is to look around your neighborhood for houses where construction work is in progress. If you are unable to find contractors through these sources, you can contact companies that advertise in local newspapers or the telephone directory.

Implementing a Competitive Bidding System

Conducting the Initial Interview

For extensive renovation work, I recommend that you establish a competitive bidding system. This involves interviewing and obtaining estimates from three to five contractors and will help to ensure that you have a wider range of experienced professionals and prices to choose from. A competitive bidding system also encourages contractors to give you their best prices because they know that other contractors will be giving you prices as well. The following questions can help you gauge the knowledge and experience of the contractors you are considering.

Is the contractor licensed? Many states have licensing requirements for contractors who perform work on residential and commercial buildings within the state. Check with your local Department of Consumer Affairs, Better Business Bureau, and/or attorney general's office to find out if licensing requirements have been adopted for contractors in your state. If so, ask if the agency can provide information concerning any complaints that have been filed against the contractors that you are obtaining bids from.

Is the contractor insured? In the event that the contractor or the contractor's employees have an accident or are injured while they are working on your property, the contractor should carry worker's compensation and liability insurance coverage for himself and his employees. Many contractors also purchase insurance policies to protect their tools and their equipment. As a final precaution, confirm that you have coverage, either through your own insurance policy or through the contractor's insurance, that protects you in the event that the contractor accidentally causes damage to the premises (e.g., fire, structural collapse, or flood) while performing the work.

How long has the contractor been in business? There really is no substitute for skill and experience. Contractors who have been in business for a long period of time have had a chance to learn the best, quickest, and most efficient ways to perform their work.

Has the contractor performed work similar to the work you want done? Contractors who are experienced in one facet of home improvements, such as roofing, may not have a great deal of experience in other areas, such as installing Sheetrock and painting. Although they may be willing to try to do the work for you, you would be better off finding contractors who have experience with the specific repairs that you require.

Can you visit the contractor's current job site to look at the work in progress? If the contractor is currently working on someone else's property, you can learn a lot by visiting the premises and seeing the quality of the contractor's work for yourself. If possible, ask the homeowner about the contractor's work habits, reliability, and professionalism. Is the contractor complying with the time frame and prices that he or she and the homeowner originally agreed to? Has the contractor asked the homeowner for extra money beyond the contractual amount, even though the homeowner hasn't asked for extra work? (It is also a good idea to ask the homeowner if the contractor is a relative. If so, there is a strong likelihood that the homeowner's opinion is somewhat biased and may not be exactly accurate.)

Can the contractor provide a current credit report? A credit report will have information about the contractor's financial position and will include claims or judgments from previous customers or unpaid suppliers against the contractor's company or against him or her individually.

In cases where extensive renovation work is planned and thousands of dollars are at stake, you may want to consider establishing an escrow account whereby you deposit money into the escrow account in contractually agreed-upon increments to ensure that the funds necessary to pay for the work will be available for the contractor. Upon written notification from you that the work is complete and that the conditions for releasing the funds have been met, the escrow agent releases the funds to the contractor from the account.

Will the contractor be hiring subcontractors? The contractor you hire may not be experienced in all of the areas of repair that you need, and will therefore hire subcontractors for this purpose. You have no control over the subcontractors that the contractor hires; however, you can certainly inquire about their level of experience and ask for proof that they are licensed and insured.

Preparing the Bid Package for Estimates

The specifications.   No matter how skilled a contractor is, the homeowner will not be satisfied if the work is not performed in accordance with his or her specifications, and it is my experience that even the best, most reputable contractors are not mind readers. For this reason, it is in the best interests of both parties for the homeowner to communicate his or her specific needs by providing the contractor with a clear description of the work the homeowner wants the contractor to do.

In order to accomplish this, the homeowner fills out and provides the contractors with a bid specification worksheet (Figures 13-1 through 13-10), which is an itemized list of the specific work that the homeowner wants the contractors to provide prices for. The bid specifications are prepared on a room-by-room basis, with each room having its own page.

This means that a property owner who wants renovation work completed in all three bedrooms in his or her three-bedroom house would prepare bid specifications for each of the three bedrooms. Similarly, if work is also required in two bathrooms, the property owner prepares two "bathroom" bid specification worksheets, one for each bathroom, and so on.

A bid specification worksheet has two components: a place to list/describe the work (for the property owner to fill out), and a column for the price (for the contractor to fill out). If the homeowner is uncertain as to what structural repairs are needed, he or she can ask the contractors who are bidding on the work for their recommendations based on their knowledge and experience.

On major reconstruction projects, if a more detailed analysis is required, the homeowner can hire a structural engineer who specializes in residential property to prepare a report.

It is sometimes a little tricky for the contractors to distinguish one room from another—especially in a vacant house with several bedrooms that are similar in size and dimension. We do not want to identify the rooms by the existing colors if we are going to repaint, or, for that matter, by the existing floor coverings if we are going to recarpet. In these circumstances I have found it helpful to assign numbers to similar rooms in the house. You can thumbtack a piece of paper on the doorways with the words "bathroom 1," "bathroom 2," "bedroom 1," "bedroom 2," "bedroom 3," and so on.

The bid specification worksheets should match the signs on the doorways (i.e., "bathroom 1," "bathroom 2," "bedroom 1," and so on) so that the contractors can provide the estimates for work on the correct rooms.

The pages that follow are examples of blank bid specification worksheets for homeowners to fill out with a description of the work that they want the contractors to give them prices for.

Figure 13-1 is an example of a blank bid specification worksheet for performing work on the exterior of the property. Figure 13-2 is an example of a blank bid specification worksheet for a kitchen. Figure 13-3 is an example of a blank bid specification worksheet for a bedroom. Figure 13-4 is an example of a blank bid specification worksheet for a bathroom. Figure 13-5 is an example of a blank bid specification worksheet for a living room. Figure 13-6 is an example of a blank bid specification worksheet for a dining room. Figure 13-7 is an example of a blank bid specification worksheet for a hallway. Figure 13-8 is an example of a blank bid specification worksheet for plumbing, heating, and electrical work. Figure 13-9 is an example of a blank bid specification worksheet for miscellaneous work that was not covered under the "room" or "exterior" categories (e.g., the removal of junk cars or other

Bid Specification Worksheet (Blank)

EXTERIOR   **PRICE**

ROOF: _____ $_____

SIDING: _____ $_____

LEADERS: _____ $_____

GUTTERS: _____ $_____

EXTERIOR PAINT: _____ $_____

WINDOWS: _____ $_____

YARD CLEANUP: _____ $_____

FENCING: _____ $_____

CEMENT WORK: _____ $_____

SHUTTERS: _____ $_____

STORMS/SCREENS: _____ $_____

EXTERIOR DOORS: _____ $_____

LANDSCAPING: _____ $_____

LIGHTING: _____ $_____

OTHER: _____ $_____

OTHER: _____ $_____

TOTAL: $_____

Figure 13-1. Bid specification worksheet—exterior work.

Bid Specification Worksheet (Blank)

KITCHEN   **PRICE**

DIMENSIONS:

FLOORING: _____ $_____

PAINTING: _____ $_____

SPACKLING: _____ $_____

WINDOWS: _____ $_____

WALL COVERING: _____ $_____

DOORS: _____ $_____

STOVE/OVEN: _____ $_____

REFRIGERATOR: _____ $_____

OTHER APPLIANCES: _____ $_____

CABINETS: _____ $_____

COUNTERS: _____ $_____

PLUMBING: _____ $_____

ELECTRICAL: _____ $_____

LIGHTING FIXTURES: _____ $_____

OTHER: _____ $_____

OTHER: _____ $_____

TOTAL: $_____

Figure 13-2. Bid specification worksheet—kitchen.

Bid Specification Worksheet (Blank)

BEDROOM #1   <u>PRICE</u>

DIMENSIONS:

FLOORING: _____ $_____

WALL COVERING: _____ $_____

PAINTING: _____ $_____

SPACKLING: _____ $_____

CLOSETS: _____ $_____

ELECTRICAL: _____ $_____

HEATING: _____ $_____

WINDOWS: _____ $_____

ENTRY DOOR: _____ $_____

CLOSET DOOR: _____ $_____

LIGHTING FIXTURES: _____ $_____

OTHER: _____ $_____

OTHER: _____ $_____

OTHER: _____ $_____

OTHER: _____ $_____

OTHER: _____ $_____

TOTAL: $_____

Figure 13-3. Bid specification worksheet—bedroom.

Bid Specification Worksheet (Blank)

BATHROOM #1	PRICE
DIMENSIONS:	
FLOORING: _____	$_____
WALL COVERING: _____	$_____
PAINTING: _____	$_____
SPACKLING: _____	$_____
CLOSETS: _____	$_____
ELECTRICAL: _____	$_____
HEATING: _____	$_____
WINDOWS: _____	$_____
ENTRY DOOR: _____	$_____
CLOSET DOOR: _____	$_____
SINK: _____	$_____
LIGHTING FIXTURES: _____	$_____
TOILET: _____	$_____
SHOWER DOORS: _____	$_____
BATHTUB: _____	$_____
OTHER: _____	$_____
TOTAL:	$_____

Figure 13-4. Bid specification worksheet—bathroom.

Bid Specification Worksheet (Blank)

LIVING ROOM   <u>PRICE</u>

DIMENSIONS:

FLOORING: _____ $_____

WALL COVERING: _____ $_____

PAINTING: _____ $_____

SPACKLING: _____ $_____

CLOSETS: _____ $_____

ELECTRICAL: _____ $_____

HEATING: _____ $_____

WINDOWS: _____ $_____

ENTRY DOOR: _____ $_____

CLOSET DOOR: _____ $_____

LIGHTING FIXTURES: _____ $_____

OTHER:_____ $_____

OTHER:_____ $_____

OTHER:_____ $_____

OTHER:_____ $_____

OTHER:_____ $_____

TOTAL: $_____

Figure 13-5.   Bid specification worksheet—living room.

Bid Specification Worksheet (Blank)

DINING ROOM	PRICE

DIMENSIONS:

FLOORING: _____ $_____

WALL COVERING: _____ $_____

PAINTING: _____ $_____

SPACKLING: _____ $_____

CLOSETS: _____ $_____

ELECTRICAL: _____ $_____

HEATING: _____ $_____

WINDOWS: _____ $_____

ENTRY DOOR: _____ $_____

CLOSET DOOR: _____ $_____

LIGHTING FIXTURES: _____ $_____

OTHER: _____ $_____

OTHER: _____ $_____

OTHER: _____ $_____

OTHER: _____ $_____

OTHER: _____ $_____

   TOTAL: $_____

Figure 13-6. Bid specification worksheet—dining room.

Bid Specification Worksheet (Blank)

HALLWAY   **PRICE**

DIMENSIONS:

LOCATION:

FLOORING: _____ $____

WALL COVERING: _____ $____

PAINTING: _____ $____

SPACKLING: _____ $____

CLOSETS: _____ $____

ELECTRICAL: _____ $____

HEATING: _____ $____

WINDOWS: _____ $____

ENTRY DOOR: _____ $____

CLOSET DOOR: _____ $____

LIGHTING FIXTURES: _____ $____

OTHER: _____ $____

OTHER: _____ $____

OTHER: _____ $____

OTHER: _____ $____

TOTAL: $_____

Figure 13-7. Bid specification worksheet—hallway.

Bid Specification Worksheet (Blank)

TYPE OF WORK (PLEASE CHECK ONE)

( ) PLUMBING WORK

( ) HEATING WORK

( ) ELECTRICAL WORK

(Include Separate Worksheets for Each Category Listed Above)

PLEASE ITEMIZE BY ROOM OR BY ENTIRE JOB:

PRICE

_____ $_____

_____ $_____

_____ $_____

_____ $_____

_____ $_____

_____ $_____

_____ $_____

_____ $_____

_____ $_____

_____ $_____

_____ $_____

_____ $_____

TOTAL: $_____

Figure 13-8. Bid specification worksheet—plumbing/heating/electrical work.

Bid Specification Worksheet (Blank)

MISCELLANEOUS   **PRICE**

(PLEASE USE FOR WORK THAT DOES NOT FALL INTO OTHER ROOM CATEGORIES)

_____ $_____

_____ $_____

_____ $_____

_____ $_____

_____ $_____

_____ $_____

_____ $_____

_____ $_____

_____ $_____

_____ $_____

_____ $_____

_____ $_____

_____ $_____

_____ $_____

_____ $_____

TOTAL: $_____

Figure 13-9. Bid specification worksheet—miscellaneous.

Bid Specification Worksheet

EXTERIOR   **PRICE**

ROOF: _Replace broken shingles where needed_ $_____

SIDING: _Paint white with brown trim (Need samples)_ $_____

LEADERS: _Install new leaders where needed_ $_____

GUTTERS: _Install new gutters where needed_ $_____

EXTERIOR PAINT: _See "siding" above_ $_____

WINDOWS: _Replace broken living room window_ $_____

YARD CLEANUP: _____ $_____

FENCING: _Remove left side_ $_____

CEMENT WORK: _____ $_____

SHUTTERS: _Paint to match brown trim_ $_____

STORMS/SCREENS: _Replace front entry storm door (Provide brochure)_ $_____

EXTERIOR DOORS: _____ $_____

LANDSCAPING: _Remove damaged tree from front lawn_ $_____

LIGHTING: _____ $_____

OTHER: _____ $_____

OTHER: _____ $_____

TOTAL: $_____

Figure 13-10. Bid specification worksheet completed by owner—exterior.

debris from the property). Figure 13-10 is an example of a completed bid specification worksheet for work on the exterior of the house.

The homeowner fills out the bid specification worksheet with a description of the work he or she wants prices for, and each contractor is given a copy and asked to fill in the prices for the items listed.

The notice to bidders. Figure 13-11 is an example of a notice to bidders form, which, like the bid specification worksheet, can be customized for your particular needs. The following paragraphs explain the information that should be included in the form.

The contractor's name and contact information. When several contractors are bidding on your job, this information helps you distinguish one contractor's estimate from another contractor's estimate.

The homeowners' names and contact numbers. This information helps the contractor to know how to reach you. It is also a good idea to indicate the best times to call.

Property address and directions. This information will help the contractor locate the correct property.

Access for entry to the premises. You have to arrange for the contractors to get inside and inspect the property so that they can prepare their estimates. The answers to the following questions will help you organize the manner in which the contractors are given access to the property. If you are living in the house now, will you schedule appointments with each of the contractors to let them in, or will you delegate that task to someone else? If the property is vacant, will you give the contractors a key and let them go there by themselves, or do you prefer to meet each of them there at different times that you can schedule in advance? If the property is currently occupied by tenants, you will have to set up appointments with the tenants for the contractors to have access.

Systems status. If possible, let the contractors know the present condition of the heating, ventilating, and air-conditioning systems so that they can bring extra equipment with them, if necessary. For example, if the electrical system is not working, the contractors who are bidding on the job may need to bring a generator or some other energy source with them in order to test the systems and prepare their estimates for the work you want done. Any other systems with an electrical tie-in (such as an oil heating system) may also be affected.

Let the contractors know if there has been a recent fuel delivery, or if they will have to provide the fuel that they need to start up the heating system and test it. If you have purchased a foreclosure in a state with a cold climate in the winter months, and the heating system was winterized to prevent the pipes from freezing, the system will have to be

NOTICE TO BIDDERS

CONTRACTOR'S NAME:_____ DATE:_____

HOMEOWNER'S NAME(S): _____

HOMEOWNER'S CONTACT NUMBER(S):

    NAME: _____   (   )_____

    NAME: _____   (   )_____

PROPERTY ADDRESS: _____

_____

DIRECTIONS TO THE PROPERTY: _____

_____

_____

ACCESS FOR ENTRY: _____

SYSTEMS STATUS:

    Electric: On   Off   Date: _____

    Heating: Oil delivered   Not operating _____

    Winterized: Yes   No   Date: _____

ADDITIONAL INSTRUCTIONS: _____

_____

_____

DEADLINE FOR COMPLETING BID SHEETS: _____

(PLEASE NOTE: BIDS RECEIVED AFTER THIS DATE AND TIME ARE DISQUALIFIED.)

Figure 13-11. A notice-to-bidders form.

dewinterized so that, if necessary, the contractors can prepare their estimates to repair the heating system.

Additional instructions. Advise the contractors if you have any requirements or deadlines for beginning and completing the work so that they can ensure that your work fits into their existing work schedule.

It is also a good idea to let the contractors know your intentions for the use of the property. If you purchased it to rent out to tenants, you will most likely have different needs from those you will have if you are planning to live there with your family. For example, an investor who plans to rent the property to tenants will most likely prefer that the contractors install commercial-quality carpeting to help make the premises as maintenance-free as possible. On the other hand, a property owner who will be moving into the house with his or her family may prefer a three-inch plush carpet, tile, granite, or hardwood floors.

You should make it clear that the specifications you have provided are by no means all-inclusive, and request the contractors to add any repairs that you may have missed (and the costs involved) directly to the bid sheet for that room.

If the work that the contractors perform will require a certificate of occupancy or similar documentation as evidence that the work was completed in compliance with the local building codes, this should also be noted so that the contractors can allow extra time for inspections by town officials when they calculate the length of time it will take them to complete the job.

Deadline for bidding. Advise the contractors of the deadline for returning their completed bid sheets to you. Deadlines help prevent bid sheets from sitting in the glove compartment of the contractors' trucks waiting to be filled out.

The bid summary sheet. The final document in the bid package is the bid summary sheet. After the contractors complete the bid specification worksheets, they should prepare a bid summary sheet listing the final prices for each room and the total price for the job. Figure 13-12 is an example of a bid summary sheet.

Each contractor must include the date on which the job will be started and completed. If you intend to rent the property to tenants, the time it takes to complete the repairs is important. Depending on the extent of the work, you may not be able to have a tenant move into the premises until the work is complete, which will affect your ability to collect rental income. Thus, an investor who is waiting to rent out the premises may consider the completion date to be as important as the prices for repairs. The investor may even select a contractor that charges a couple of hundred dollars more than the other contractors because

BID SUMMARY SHEET

PROPERTY ADDRESS: _____

CONTRACTOR'S NAME: _____

CONTRACTOR'S ADDRESS: _____

CONTRACTOR'S TELEPHONE NUMBER: _____

TOTAL PRICE OF JOB: $ _____

DATE WORK WILL BEGIN: _____

DATE OF COMPLETION: _____

ROOM/SYSTEM   **PRICE**

Exterior: _____ $_____

Kitchen: _____ $_____

Bedroom 1: _____ $_____

Bedroom 2: _____ $_____

Bedroom 3: _____ $_____

Living Room: _____ $_____

Dining Room: _____ $_____

Bathroom 1: _____ $_____

Bathroom 2: _____ $_____

Hallway: _____ $_____

Plumbing: _____ $_____

Heating: _____ $_____

Electric: _____ $_____

   TOTAL JOB: $_____

Figure 13-12. A bid summary sheet.

that contractor is able to complete the job a month earlier. (Under those circumstances, the extra couple of hundred dollars it will cost the investor is more than offset by [let's say] a $1,800 monthly rental payment.)

On the other hand, if you are buying the foreclosure to live in, and the time of completion is not a material factor, you might select the contractor with the lowest prices—even if that contractor requires more time to complete the work than the other contractors.

Check to make sure that the contractor has included prices for all of the bid specification worksheets, including the plumbing, heating, and electrical systems worksheet and the miscellaneous page (if applicable). It is also a good idea to check the contractor's calculations for each room.

Setting Up a Comparative Cost Analysis Worksheet

After the contractors return their completed estimates, you can set up a worksheet that allows you to compare "apples to apples." Figure 13-13 is an example of a comparative cost analysis worksheet that you can use to compare and contrast the contractors' estimates.

Look for prices that are dramatically higher or lower than the prices given by the other contractors. For example, if one contractor's price for the carpeting in bedroom 1 is a lot less than the prices given to you by the other contractors, the reason may be that the contractor will be installing an inferior carpet. On the other hand, the contractor with the low price may have a supply of high-quality carpet left over from the last job that he or she completed and be passing the savings on to you. To avoid problems of this nature, whenever possible, provide the contractors with samples of the carpet (and the padding) that you want installed. Also provide as much information as possible about the color, manufacturer, and so on to make it easier for the contractors to get prices.

If you do not have a particular product or color scheme in mind, you can request that the contractors provide you with samples of the flooring material (carpet, padding, tiles, wood, or linoleum), wall coverings (tile, wallpaper, paint, or paneling), exterior siding materials (aluminum, vinyl, wood, or shingles), roof shingles, and so forth, that they are basing their estimates on. Request samples of paint colors. (There are hundreds of shades of white.) Ask the contractors to provide you with brochures for appliances (e.g., are the prices based on rebuilt models rather than brand new ones?) and for plumbing and electrical fixtures, so that you can see the quality of the items the contractors are giving you prices for.

Job Total			Date Begin (1)	Complete Date (2)	Exterior (3)	Bedrm #1 (4)	Bedrm #2 (5)	Bedrm #3 (6)	Living Room (7)	Dining Room (8)	Bath #1 (9)	etc. (10)
Contractor #1												
Contractor #2												
Contractor #3												
Contractor #4												
Contractor #5												

Figure 13-13. A comparative cost analysis worksheet.

Awarding the Job

When you are satisfied that you have obtained prices for all of the work, select the contractor who can do the job within the time frame and budget that is most beneficial for you. Meet with the contractor, go over the bid results, and finalize the prices and completion date. The next step is to negotiate a payment plan that recognizes everyone's priorities.

Implementing a Performance-Based Payment Plan

Depending on the size of the job and the length of time it will take to complete, there are several options for paying a contractor. Some contractors prefer to be paid in three equal installments—one installment at the start of the job, one installment at the midpoint, and the final payment upon completion of the job. Other contractors prefer to receive half of the amount due when they start the job and the other half when they complete it. Unfortunately, problems can—and often do—arise in which one party's actions harm the other party. One classic example is when the contractor gets paid up front, then disappears with the property owner's money (or goes out of business), and never returns to complete the work. This could cause a considerable amount of hardship for the homeowner, who may have given the contractor all of his or her savings and be unable to afford to pay someone else to complete the work. The only remedy available may be a lawsuit in the civil courts, which can take years to come to trial. And even if the homeowner is awarded a judgment against the contractor, it could be difficult to find any assets to seize, especially if the contractor has gone bankrupt or moved away without leaving a forwarding address. Many states have adopted contractor's licensing requirements to maintain high standards in the industry and to eliminate fraudulent practices. Some states may also have established a fund that they use to help reimburse homeowners who were defrauded by dishonest contractors.

On the other side of the coin, the homeowner who is having the work done might not have enough money to pay the contractor after the work has been completed. Needless to say, this could be disastrous for the contractor, who has already laid out a lot of money for labor and materials on that job and needs to be reimbursed.

The payment policy that I have found to be most effective is for the contractor to be paid on a weekly basis for the work that was completed during the previous week. Here is how it works. Each week, on an agreed-upon day, the contractor calls the property owner with a list of the repairs that the contractor intends to complete by the end of the week. As a result, the property owner knows in advance the anticipated progress of the work and how much of a payment he or she will have to make at the end of the week. On the designated inspection day, the property owner inspects the work that was performed and pays the contractor the price that the contractor assigned to that work on the bid specification worksheet. For example, if the contractor gave the property owner a price of $250 for carpeting and $100 for painting in bedroom 1, and those items were inspected and confirmed to be complete, the property owner would pay the contractor $350.

The property owner benefits because a performance-based agreement inherently encourages expeditious results, and since the payment is made only after the work is completed, the owner is less vulnerable to a contractor's fraud. The contractor benefits because he or she does not have to wait long periods of time to be reimbursed for work that was completed and can count on steady weekly paychecks.

The property owner and the contractor must keep track of the payments made as the work progresses. In order to avoid accidentally paying for the same work more than once, both parties should keep copies of the checks paid to the contractor, and the dates and check numbers should be written in the margins next to each item on the bid sheet as that item is paid.

Establishing an Escrow Account

Another way in which funds can be controlled is by setting up an escrow account. An escrow account assures the contractor that the property owner has the funds available to pay him or her for the work.

The property owner deposits into the escrow account an amount of money that was contractually agreed upon at the time when the job was awarded to the contractor. An escrow agent (usually an attorney or a mediator) is selected and given specific instructions as to the conditions that must be met in order for funds to be released from the escrow account. The escrow agent is charged with releasing the funds to the contractor in accordance with those instructions.

Your attorney, accountant, and/or financial advisor should be contacted for assistance in setting up an escrow account and determining the payment terms that will best suit your needs.

Developing the Contractor's Agreement

A well-defined contractor's agreement plays an essential role in helping property owners and contractors protect themselves when work is performed on a foreclosure.

As in any transaction, the agreement should be set forth in writing, and its terms should meet the expectations of both parties. Any fee that you pay to have the agreement drawn up can save you thousands of dollars down the line because litigation is less likely to arise in situations where the terms of an agreement are clearly defined. Be sure to include the amount you have agreed to pay, the payment dates, and the terms you have agreed upon. Also of importance are the dates on which the work will begin and end and the default remedies in the event that the repairs are not completed in a timely manner. In states that require contractors to be licensed, the property owner should have a copy of the contractor's license that was issued by the state, and should have proof of insurance coverage. A copy of the final bid specification worksheet and the bid summary sheet with the start and completion dates should be attached as a rider to the agreement as well.

Figure 13-14 is a sample contractor's agreement. This agreement is just a sample of the terms and conditions that could be included. You should contact your attorney for more information about the state-specific terms and conditions that are applicable in your situation.

When drafting the agreement consider including these terms and conditions:

Other Contract Terms to Include

Penalties for late completion. The contract should stipulate the penalties that will be assessed against the contractor if the work is completed after the agreed-upon deadline. You may have chosen this contractor because he or she promised an earlier completion date than other contractors, even though the price was a little higher than the prices the others submitted. If the job is unjustifiably delayed by the contractor, you should not be penalized by having to pay the premium price this contractor charged you if you no longer have the benefit of the earlier completion date. If the contractor knows in advance that there will be stiff penalties assessed for every day the job is delayed past the agreed-upon deadline, that contractor will be more motivated to finish your job on time.

If you are an investor, you can base the penalty amount on the rental income you are losing because your tenant was unable to move in until the repairs were completed. For example, if your property has an expected monthly rental income of $1,800, you could set the penalty amount at $60 per day for each day that the work was incomplete after the agreed-upon deadline. On the other hand, if you live in the house (or will be living in the house after the repairs are complete), you can base the penalty on your monthly loan payment, which must be paid to your lender every month whether you are living in the house or not.

PROPERTY OWNER AND CONTRACTOR AGREEMENT

This agreement is made this _____ day of _____ 20____ by and between
_____, hereinafter called the homeowner and _____, hereinafter called the
contractor.

For the consideration hereinafter named, the homeowner and the contractor agree as follows:

The Work: The contractor agrees to furnish all material and perform all work necessary to complete
the repairs to the property located at: _____, in accordance with the specifications given
by the homeowner and attached herewith.

The Time: The contractor agrees to promptly begin work as agreed to, and to complete the work as
follows: Work to begin: _____ Date of completion: _____

A Penalty for work completed past the deadline will be assessed in the amount of $_____ per day.

Extras: No deviation from the work or material specified in the specifications will be permitted or
paid for unless a written work or change order is first agreed upon and signed as required.

Assignment: No assignment of this contract agreement is permitted without prior written permission
from the homeowner.

Subcontractors: The contractor agrees to inform the homeowner about any subcontractors who will be
hired by the contractor to perform on the job. The contractor agrees to provide the homeowner with any
proofs of insurance or any other qualifications of any subcontractors who will be working on the job.

Insurance: The contractor agrees to obtain and pay for the following insurance coverage: worker's
compensation, public liability, property damage, and any other insurance coverage that may be necessary or
required by the homeowner or by state or law.

Taxes: The contractor agrees to pay any and all federal, state, or local taxes that are, or may be,
assessed upon the material and labor that are furnished under this contract.

Payment: The homeowner agrees to pay the contractor, for materials and work, the sum of
$_____. A ____% retainage will be deducted from each payment to the contractor.

Payment terms, amounts, and dates, are agreed upon as follows: <u>ATTACH BID SPECIFICATIONS
WITH FINAL PRICES AND BID SUMMARY SHEET.</u>

The homeowner and the contractor, for themselves, their successors, executors, administrators, and
assignees, hereby agree to the full performance of the covenants herein contained.

DATE:_____   DATE:_____

_____   _____
Property Owner's Name   Contractor's Name

_____   _____
Property Owner's Signature   Contractor's Signature

Figure 13-14. A sample contractor's agreement.

Accordingly, your daily penalty amount can be calculated using the number of days in an average month (i.e., one-thirtieth of your monthly loan costs) for every day the job is delayed past the agreed-upon deadline.

Rewards for early completion. A recent trend has emerged whereby contractors are offered rewards for early completion of projects such as widening of highways, repairing of bridges, and so on. Just as the threat of penalties is a powerful motivator, a reward for early completion has proven to be motivational as well. An early-completion reward is another option to include in your agreement when the time frame for completion is of great importance.

Extensions of deadlines. Sometimes unforeseen disasters, such as hurricanes, tornadoes, or other weather conditions, cause delays that render the contractual deadline unrealistic. It is helpful to spell out in your original agreement with the contractor what you *would* and *would not* consider acceptable as reasons for delays, and to incorporate the distinction between "reasonable" and "unreasonable" delays into your agreement. Additional work requested by the property owner that was not included in the original specifications could also cause work to extend past the deadline. A specific time limit should be agreed to in writing whenever additional work is requested. If necessary, an extension should be granted (in writing). Figure 13-15 is an extension form for expanding the time frame to complete repairs without any penalties to the contractor. The form is not all-inclusive, and you should consult an attorney for state-specific terms that are applicable for your situation.

Waiver of mechanic's lien. Contractors working close to the financial edge may use the money you paid them for the work they performed on your foreclosure to pay for materials that they purchased for a previous job. If the contractor does not pay for the materials purchased for your job, you may find that a mechanic's lien was filed against your home. A mechanic's lien is a statutory financial claim against property that is created in favor of contractors, laborers, and/or suppliers who have performed work or furnished materials to erect or repair a building and were not paid. I have heard horror stories from property owners who discovered that liens had been filed against their homes by building supply companies, even though the property owners had paid the contractors in full for their jobs. You can help protect yourself by asking the contractor, as part of your contract terms, to provide you with a "waiver of mechanic's lien rights" for any subcontractors or material suppliers who provided labor or materials for your job. Contact your attorney for more information about protecting yourself from this heavy-duty headache.

Extension of Deadline to Complete Work

DATE OF EXTENSION: _____

PROPERTY ADDRESS: _____

REASON FOR EXTENSION REQUEST: _____

ORIGINAL CONTRACT DEADLINE: _____

EXTENSION REQUESTED: _____

NEW CONTRACT DEADLINE: _____

AGREED TO:

(Date)_____   (Date)_____

_____   _____
Property Owner's Signature   Contractor's Signature

Figure 13-15. A sample contractor's extension form.

Holding back a retainage. Another way in which property owners protect themselves financially is to hold back a percentage of the amount owed, called a "retainage," from each payment check. Thus, in the example given earlier where the contractor received payment in the amount of $350 for the painting and carpeting work completed in bedroom 1, you would hold back an agreed-upon retainage (e.g., 10 percent) from each payment made to the contractor. So, in this example, you would hold back $35, and the contractor would be paid $315. This may not seem like a lot of money now, but if the repair costs amount to thousands of dollars, the retainage you hold becomes much more significant. The retainage is usually released as the final payment to the contractor after all punch list items have been completed in accordance with the terms of your agreement.

The final release of the retainage to the contractor can be contingent upon several things. For example, if the contractor is to provide you with a certificate of occupancy or its equivalent, then the retainage can be held back until the contractor provides you with that document. Retainage money can also be used by a property owner to hire a new contractor to complete a repair that the original contractor did incorrectly, or it can be applied toward damages stipulated in the contract if work was not completed in a timely manner. Retainage may also be held back from payments when you want to make certain that the plumbing, heating, or electrical systems that the contractor has just finished working on continue to operate properly over a period of a few days. The percent of retainage that will be deducted from each check should be agreed to as part of the contract terms.

Frequency of inspections and payments for completed work. Be as specific as possible about the dates and times for inspections that will be performed in order for the contractor to be paid. The frequency of inspections and payments must be clearly defined, and so should the conditions that must be met for the retainage to be released to the contractor by the property owner.

The Big Picture

Whether you use all of these suggestions, some of them, or none, the most important thing is that the agreement you create meets the needs of each party. Ultimately, the best agreement is one where, at the end of its term, the homeowner and the contractor walk away with a great feeling that something wonderful was accomplished.

14

Getting Started Today

Together we have looked at the benefits and risks involved in buying real estate foreclosures. The benefits are maximized and the risks are diminished when you put your time and effort into learning the foreclosure-purchasing procedure and applying what you've learned toward fulfilling your dreams. In Chapter 14, we start you on your journey with six simple steps to help you turn your dreams into reality today.

Follow These Six Steps for Success in Purchasing Foreclosures

Step 1: Arrange Your Financing

If you will need financing in order to purchase your foreclosure, begin the procedure for getting your preapproval now. The loan officer at your lending institution will let you know how much you can borrow based on your current income and credit rating. (See "Calculating Your Foreclosure Budget" in Chapter 6.)

If you have equity built up in the house you currently own and reside in, you can begin the procedure for obtaining an equity loan, a refinance, or a junior lien to finance your foreclosure. Chapter 6 helps you prepare a spreadsheet to use for comparing the financing terms that are offered by lending institutions. From there, you can select the loan with the best terms for your current needs and future goals.

Alternatively, if you know people who have the money to buy a foreclosure but who have limited time to perform the necessary legwork, think about purchasing with partners for now. You can offer your expertise as your contribution, or if you have some funds of your own available, you can contribute a portion of the funds to the transaction in return for a larger share of the equity stake in the property, as discussed in Chapter 8.

Another option to consider is an equity-sharing arrangement in which your role will be that of either the "insider" or the "investor." (See Chapter 8 for a complete discussion of this subject.)

Step 2: Develop Your Network of Support

You will need to find an attorney who is knowledgeable about foreclosure procedures to help answer your questions and protect your interests. Contact your local bar association and ask for a list of attorneys in your area who specialize in real estate or foreclosure matters. Ask the attorneys you contact for the fees they charge for their services before you hire them. Also ask for client referrals that you can contact for references. It is very important that you contact these clients to see if they were satisfied with the services that the attorney provided. Is the attorney always accessible, or will you have to wait two weeks for your phone call to be returned? Was the attorney knowledgeable about all phases of the foreclosure-purchasing process? Does the attorney handle evictions? Because the fees and services provided by different attorneys will vary, I suggest that you contact several attorneys (and their client references) in order to develop a more accurate basis for comparison.

You will need an accountant or a financial advisor who can review your specific financial situation and recommend the best monetary plan of action for you to pursue. Your friends or relatives may be able to recommend someone to you, and many certified public accountants and financial advisors advertise in the local telephone directory. Ask for information about the fees they charge for their services. Also, ask for people you can call for references, as you did when you were looking for an attorney.

You will need a reputable licensed contractor or engineer to assist you with your repair needs. Ask for references and photographs of the work the contractor or engineer has completed in the past. Contact your local consumer affairs office (or its equivalent) to confirm that the contractor or engineer is licensed with the appropriate government agency and to ensure that no complaints have been filed against the company or the individual.

You will need an insurance expert. Although the fees for some types of insurance are governed by state law, costs for other types of insurance vary. With the assistance of an insurance expert, you can select insurance coverage that protects your interests as a landlord or as an owner-occupant at prices that fit your budget.

Step 3: Send for Your Foreclosure Lists

If you have decided to purchase your foreclosure at an auction, review Chapter 2 for the details concerning this opportunity, and send away for lists of upcoming auctions.

Chapter 3 is a great resource if you are interested in buying a bank-owned REO foreclosure after the auction. Begin by contacting lenders with REOs in your area and asking them to send you lists of the properties in their inventories.

If you wish to pursue purchasing your REO foreclosure from a government agency, such as the DVA, HUD, GSA, or FDIC, you can review the techniques for ordering lists of government-owned properties in Chapter 4.

If you want to buy a preforeclosure before the auction, the sources and strategies detailed in Chapter 5 can help you contact and negotiate with defaulting borrowers.

Step 4: Review Your Foreclosure Facts

Review the information contained in this book on a daily basis until the procedures and the success that will result have become a part of you. Remember, repetition is the mother of learning. Review the checklists and the step-by-step activities, and then picture your success in your mind.

Step 5: Select the Properties That Are Right for You and Do a Trial Run

Select the properties that are right for you, contact the appropriate parties, and ask the prebid questions (from Chapter 9) about the properties you are interested in. Inspect the premises and prepare your bid sheet as discussed in Chapter 10. I suggest that you attend several auctions in order to experience the actual procedure in person and to verify how you would have done if you had actually bid on the property. In so doing, you will build up your confidence as you learn to trust your own judgment. (Please note, however, that trial runs are recommended only up to the bidding point. Referees, sheriffs, and trustees will get rather cranky if you call out a bogus offer because you forgot that this was just a trial run and got caught up in the bidding!)

Step 6: Don't Give Up

No one has ever achieved success by quitting. Ben Franklin tried hundreds of times before he discovered electricity. Thank goodness he

GETTING STARTED TODAY

( ) **Step 1.** Arrange your financing.

( ) **Step 2.** Develop your network of support.

( ) **Step 3.** Send away for the lists of upcoming foreclosure sales.

( ) **Step 4.** Review your foreclosure information daily until the procedure and the success you will have becomes a part of you.

( ) **Step 5.** Select the properties that are right for you and do a trial run.

( ) **Step 6.** Don't give up!

Not all-inclusive—additional steps may be required

Figure 14-1. A sample checklist: "getting started today."

never gave up! (And he didn't even have a book like this to get him started.) To give you an idea of how crucial a role persistence plays in success, under normal market conditions you need to contact a defaulting borrower approximately four times before you get a response. You will attempt to buy an REO 20 times before your offer for a bank- or a government-owned foreclosure is accepted. You may end up preparing 25 bids and attending 25 auctions before you are the successful high bidder.

Remember: WINNERS NEVER QUIT . . . AND QUITTERS NEVER WIN!

A checklist titled "Getting Started Today" is provided as Figure 14-1. It is not intended to be all-inclusive. You may need to obtain additional information from other sources. Further steps may be necessary, and you should customize and supplement the list with additional tasks that you must complete in accordance with your specific purchasing strategy.

From Rags to Riches with Real Estate Foreclosures

A foreclosure purchase is a great way to buy a property at a below-market price to keep as a long-term residence, or to keep as an investment property rented out to others, or to "fix up" and "flip" for a large profit. Many real estate entrepreneurs have already acquired fortunes from this type of real estate transaction. Above all, I want to leave you with the knowledge and belief that you too can become successful. I hope I have given you the tools you need that will empower you with success and help you achieve your goals.

Glossary

A

Absolute auction   An auction wherein the seller must accept the highest bid even if it is lower than the seller's preferred sales price.

Adjustable rate loans   A loan where monthly interest payments fluctuate in conjunction with the index and margin specified in the loan documents. Borrowers face the uncertainty of changeable market rates each anniversary (usually one-, three-, or five-year terms) when the rates adjust.

Asset manager   The person, entity, or real estate broker that acts as an agent for the REO seller and assists in the preparations for marketing and selling the foreclosed property from the bank or government agency's inventory.

Assumable loans   Loans that can be taken over by a purchaser who wishes to leave the existing loan intact. The purchaser pays the difference between the purchase price and the loan balance in cash, assumes the loan balance, and is responsible for making future monthly payments to the lender.

Auction with reservation   An auction wherein the seller reserves the right to reject any offer from a bidder no matter how lucrative it is.

B

Balloon loan   A loan where, at the end of its term, the entire remaining balance is due in a lump sum payment, requiring the borrower to obtain new financing to pay it off.

Bankruptcy   A legal procedure initiated by people who require a reorganization plan for debt consolidation and/or repayment of existing debt. When filed, this procedure puts a halt to creditors' attempts to collect on the unpaid obligations.

Beneficiary   When a deed of trust is the security device for a loan, the lender is the beneficiary.

Binder A deposit sent to the owner of real estate by someone who is presenting an offer to purchase the property. Unless agreed to otherwise, binders are returned to the prospective purchaser if the owner rejects the offer.

Bond A written obligation wherein the borrowers promise to repay their loans in accordance with the terms of their agreement with the lender. It is usually issued at the time of the execution of the security instrument (the mortgage or deed of trust).

C

Cash flow The money that "flows" into a rental property (i.e., rental income) and out of it (i.e., carrying charges such as the loan payment, property taxes, property insurance, repairs, maintenance). A positive cash flow is achieved when the income flowing into the property exceeds the carrying charges flowing out of the property. A negative cash flow results when carrying charges flowing out of the property exceed the income flowing in.

Certificate of Occupancy (CO) A document issued by a town, county, or local government agency's building department to certify that the dwelling and/or any improvements were constructed in compliance with the local building codes.

Closed-end home equity loans (HEL) A loan where the borrower receives a lump sum at the closing and cannot borrow additional amounts.

Complaint A plaintiff's allegations of entitlement to relief and the relief sought. In a foreclosure situation, the plaintiff is the lender.

Contract transfers Also known as *flipping the contract*, a strategy whereby a purchaser (buyer #1) successfully bids on a property at an auction and then assigns the contract to another purchaser (buyer #2) before the closing date. Buyer #2 refunds buyer #1's original down payment plus an agreed upon profit and becomes the new contract vendee. In a contract transfer, buyer #1 is still responsible for completing the transaction if buyer #2 fails to close.

Conventional fixed rate loan A loan where monthly interest payments do not fluctuate during the life of the loan.

Cram down *See* Short sale.

D

Deed in Lieu of Foreclosure An agreement between a defaulting borrower and the lender of the loan that is in default whereby the lender agrees to accept the deed (and the keys to the house) as payment in full and grants the borrower a full release from the remaining loan obligation.

Deed of trust *See* Trust deed.

Default notice A notice issued by the lender to advise the borrower to pay arrears by a certain date or the entire remaining balance will become due and payable.

Defaulting borrower A mortgagor or trustor who fails to make the loan payments as set forth in the mortgage or deed of trust. The lender may accelerate the loan payments and begin a foreclosure proceeding to sell the premises and recapture its losses by auctioning the property to the highest bidder.

Defaulting homeowner   *See* Defaulting borrower.

Deficiency judgment   A court decision obtained by a mortgagee for the amount of money still due and payable on the loan balance that the mortgagee was unable to recapture through the sale of the property at an auction. The defaulting borrower that the judgment is filed against is personally liable for paying off the remaining amount due.

Delinquent homeowner   *See* Defaulting borrower.

Department of Housing and Urban Development (HUD) foreclosures   A source of government foreclosure lists, also known as FHA foreclosures. HUD foreclosures occur when a borrower defaults and the lender forecloses on an FHA loan. HUD pays the lending institution for the outstanding loan and expenses incurred. HUD takes ownership and resells it to the public.

Depreciation   Associated with income taxes, depreciation is an investor's deduction that results from the decline in the value of real estate over time because of such factors as wear and tear and adverse changes to a neighborhood.

Dollar bid   *See* Upset price.

Down payment   When purchasing a real estate property, the difference between the purchase price and the amount of the loan that a lender will allow you to borrow to purchase the property.

E

Equity sharing   A creative financing strategy for buying foreclosures with a partner, sharing the benefits derived during the term of the agreement, and splitting the profits after the property is sold. The inside occupant lives in the house and pays the monthly carrying charges. The outside investor does not live in the house and pays for the purchase and financing costs.

Escrow account for taxes and insurance   A process whereby borrowers pay extra money each month that is deposited into a reserve account set up by a lender for the purpose of accruing funds to pay future real estate taxes and property insurance. When the payments for the property taxes and insurance premiums come due, the lender withdraws the funds from the escrow account and forwards the taxes to the tax collector and the insurance premiums to the insurance company. By ensuring the timely payment of these charges, the lender protects its interest in the property.

F

Federal Deposit Insurance Corporation (FDIC) sales   A source of government foreclosure lists, the FDIC is an independent agency of the U.S. government best known for protecting U.S. bank deposits. FDIC also functions as the receiver when a financial institution fails. The FDIC provides lists of properties from its inventory of residential and commercial property and vacant land.

Federal Home Loan Mortgage Corporation (Freddy Mac) sales   A source of government foreclosure lists, Freddy Mac is a publicly chartered agency that buys residential mortgages from lending institutions and sells the foreclosures to the public, usually through real estate brokers.

Federal National Mortgage Association (Fannie Mae) sales A source of government foreclosure lists, Fannie Mae is the largest purchaser of mortgages in the secondary market. Fannie Mae sells properties from its inventory to the public, usually through real estate brokers.

FHA foreclosures *See* Department of Housing and Urban Development (HUD) foreclosures.

FICO (Fair Isaac Corporation) score The most common measure used by lenders nationwide to determine a potential borrower's creditworthiness.

Final judgment *See* Judgment of Foreclosure and Sale.

Fixed rate loans *See* Conventional fixed rate loan.

Forbearance An agreement between a defaulting borrower and the lender whereby, depending on the circumstances surrounding the default, the lender allows the borrower to pay less than the full amount owed per month, or even allows the borrower to pay nothing for a pre-agreed period of time after which payments will resume.

Foreclosure The legal procedure initiated by a lender of a mortgage or trustee of a trust deed seeking to recapture its losses by selling the property at a public auction.

Foreclosure search A process conducted in the initial stages of a foreclosure that is similar to ordering a report from a title company. The report from the search provides the foreclosing lender's attorney with information about the property owner, mortgage, or deed of trust and junior liens attached to the premises that is vital to the foreclosure procedure.

Friendly foreclosure *See* Deed in Lieu of Foreclosure.

G

Government Services Administration (GSA) A source of government foreclosure lists, the GSA oversees the sales of real estate that was formerly used by the federal government and offers it as surplus property to the general public through a public bidding system.

Graduated payment loans Loans where the payment increases by preset amounts during the first few years and then stabilizes at a fixed interest rate. Borrowers are given the loan terms up front and are aware of the percentage that the interest rate will increase over the term of the loan.

H

Hard money loans Although different from "break your arm financing" by a loan shark, hard money lenders generally charge higher interest rates and closing costs than conventional loans.

Home equity loans A loan that allows borrowers to tap into the equity built up in a home they own to finance other interests such as major home repairs, education, medical bills, or even a down payment on another home. *Also see*

Closed end home equity loans (HEL), and/or Open-end home equity loan (HELOC).

Home Equity Theft Prevention Act (HETPA)   Laws adopted by a state to protect defaulting homeowners from losing their homes to unscrupulous scam artists who use high-pressure tactics to trick them into signing away the title to their homes. These laws usually target sales to investors. State HETPAs set forth detailed circumstances where defaulting owner-occupants have the right to cancel or rescind contracts and deeds and regain ownership of their homes within a statutory period of time.

I

Income producing   A term that describes investment property where a tenant's monthly rental payment can be applied to offset the property's carrying charges.

Index   The bank's rate of borrowing, meaning the amount that the lender is charged to put money out on the street to borrowers. Lenders all use a specific index, which is specified in the loan documents and can be followed in most newspapers. Interest rates on adjustable rate loans are recalculated on each anniversary (commonly one-, three-, or five-year terms) according to the average of the index.

Index number   A document purchased by a plaintiff, who is the lender in a foreclosure action, to bring a legal action onto the court's calendar.

Interest only loans   Loans where the borrower's payments are applied only to the interest that is due. Interest only loans provide no reduction to the principal of the loan, and the original loan amount balance is still due at the end of the loan term.

Investors   People who purchase real estate at below market prices, using as little of their own money as possible, without any intention of occupying it as a primary dwelling. Investors hold the property as an investment and rent it out to tenants whose rent payments cover the property's carrying charges thereby building equity each month for the investor, or they fix the property up and sell it quickly to earn a profit.

J

Judgment of Foreclosure and Sale   (a.k.a. final judgment) A judgment issued by the judge as the final step in a foreclosure procedure, the Judgment of Foreclosure and Sale establishes the final order for the foreclosing lender to sell the property at a public auction.

Judicial foreclosure   A court-ordered proceeding whereby a property is sold to satisfy an unpaid mortgage loan.

Junior lien   A lien that is subordinate to prior recorded liens.

L

Lien theory states   In states that have adopted the lien theory, when a property is encumbered with a mortgage, the mortgagor (borrower) is the owner of the premises and holds the title, while the mortgagee (lender) holds the first mortgage on the property.

Life cap The maximum amount that the interest rate can go up or down during the life of the adjustable rate loan (usually over a period of 15, 20, 25, or 30 years).

Lis pendens From the Latin for action pending, this legal document gives notice to the world that there is an action pending on a property which may negatively affect the title.

Loan modification An agreement between a defaulting borrower and the lender that restructures the terms of the original loan. These new terms can include lowering the interest rate, converting a high interest adjustable rate loan into a lower fixed rate loan, and lengthening the remaining term of the loan to give the borrower more time to pay off the loan and in many cases significantly reduce the monthly payments.

Loss mitigation representative Before a lender forecloses on a deed of trust or a mortgage, the loan loss mitigation department's primary objective is to pursue a settlement with the defaulting borrower that yields the highest net price possible for the lender. To accomplish this, loss mitigation representatives negotiate alternatives to foreclosure, including short sales, deeds in lieu of foreclosure, and loan modification agreements.

M

Margin The percent of profit the lender wants to earn above the index. The margin remains the same over the life of the adjustable rate loan. The index plus the margin equals the prevailing rate of interest.

Market value The highest price paid by an informed purchaser, not under duress, when the property is widely exposed on the open market.

Mechanic's lien A financial claim filed against real property by a contractor, supplier of material, or provider of services for the premises when payment was not made for the work performed. Mechanics liens are valid for a period of one year and may be renewed.

Minimum bid auction An auction where the seller establishes a starting amount to begin the bidding. All bids must exceed that amount, and the highest bidder is awarded the contract. (This is the process used for foreclosure auctions.)

Mortgage A two-party security instrument between a borrower (mortgagor) and a lender (mortgagee) whereby the mortgagor pledges the title to real property as security for the loan to ensure that it will be repaid in accordance with the terms of the promissory note.

Mortgage Debt Cancellation Relief Act Enacted by Congress on December 20, 2007, in response to the subprime loan crisis, declining property values, and an alarming number of foreclosures nationwide, this Act stipulates that defaulting borrowers who qualify will not be required to pay federal, state, city, and/or local income taxes on discharged or forgiven debt. This new law applies to mortgage debt on the borrower's principal residence that is forgiven or discharged in a short sale, a workout agreement with a lender, or a foreclosure during the time period from January 2007 through December 31, 2009.

Mortgagee   The lender of a mortgage loan that receives a mortgage from the borrower (mortgagor) pledging the property as the security for the debt.

Mortgagor   The borrower of a mortgage loan that executes and delivers a mortgage instrument to the lender (mortgagee) as security for the debt.

N

Negative amortization   The process that occurs when the prevailing rate of interest (the index plus the margin) on an adjustable rate loan exceeds the maximum term cap allowed, and the difference between the higher new payment and interest due is added to the loan balance.

Net sheet   A financial statement prepared by a defaulting borrower during short sale negotiations with a lender that sets forth the proposed sales price, the expenses that will be deducted, and the balance of the net proceeds that will be paid to the lender.

Non-income producing   Investment property where no income is produced by a tenant, but the property is used as a second home or vacation home.

Nonjudicial foreclosure   The procedure where the foreclosing mortgage lender or deed of trust beneficiary invokes the power of sale clause, allowing the lender or trustee to sell the property at a public auction without a court order.

O

Open-end home equity loan (HELOC)   A loan where the borrower is allowed a maximum draw rather than a fixed dollar amount. There is a draw period where the borrower can draw on the line of credit and a repayment period where the borrowed money has to be repaid.

Opening bid amount   *See* Upset price.

Owner-occupants   People who purchase real estate to live in as their primary residence.

P

Piggyback loans   A financing option that allows a borrower to purchase property with loans from more than one lender. The borrower is required to come up with only a very low down payment because the two loans cover most, if not all, of the purchase price.

Power of Sale clause   A provision in a loan that allows the lender to foreclose and sell the borrower's property publicly without invoking a legal procedure through the courts.

Preapproval   The process by which a lender investigates the creditworthiness of an applicant for a loan to purchase real estate before the applicant finds the property he or she wishes to purchase. The application is processed and the lender issues a commitment to lend the money provided that, when the applicant finds a property to purchase, the house appraises for enough money to satisfy the lender's guidelines and that the title to the property is clear.

Prepayment penalty A fine imposed by a lender on a borrower for paying off the loan balance before the end of the term, usually by selling the property or refinancing it with a new loan.

Prequalification The process by which a lender gives an applicant an estimate of the loan that he or she qualifies for based upon the income and credit stated by the applicant. The final application process does not begin until after the applicant finds a property to purchase, enters into the contract of sale, and formally applies for the loan.

Promissory note A written contract signed by a borrower promising to pay a specific amount of money by a definite future date.

Purchase money mortgage A mortgage given by a buyer to a seller (a traditional private seller or a lender that is providing financing for the buyer) to secure payment for part or all of the purchase price.

R
Referee The individual to whom a court refers a foreclosure action for the purpose of reporting findings of fact during the course of the procedure.

Reinstatement An agreement between a defaulting borrower and the lender for the borrower to repay the monthly amounts that are in arrears by making a lump sum payment within a pre-agreed period of time.

REO (real estate owned) Repossessed property that returns to a bank or government agency's inventory either through a Deed in Lieu of Foreclosure or if the property is not sold at the public auction.

Repayment An agreement between a defaulting borrower and the lender to repay the monthly amounts that are in arrears over an extended period of time, commonly as add-ons to the regular monthly loan payments.

Retainage During the course of construction, the amount of money held back from each payment to a contractor, usually in the form of a percentage of the payment (e.g., 10 percent). The retainage is released in a final payment to the contractor after the contractor completes the job and all punch list items.

Right of redemption Available to everyone with an ownership interest in real property, the right of redemption requires that up until the auction begins (and in some states, for a statutory period of time after the auction is completed), defaulting borrowers may buy back or reacquire the property pledged as security for the loan by paying the unpaid loan balance in full. In some cases, the lender allows the borrower to redeem the property just by paying the late loan payments.

S
Seasoning The requirement by a lender that an applicant who wishes to obtain a loan on a real estate property that the applicant already owns must

have held ownership for one or two years (i.e., a 'seasoned ownership') before the lender will grant the loan.

Sheriff The chief peace officer of a county, responsible for carrying out the judicial process in a foreclosure procedure.

Short sale An arrangement between a lender and the defaulting homeowner wherein the lender agrees to accept less than the outstanding loan balance as payment in full when the proceeds of the property sale fall short of the total amount due.

Soldier's and Sailor's Civil Relief Act of 1940 This Act states that no sale or foreclosure or seizure of property for nonpayment of any sum due will be valid when the property is owned by a serviceperson who is on active military duty and the loan was originated prior to the commencement of that military duty.

Summons Notice served in a mortgage foreclosure procedure directing the defendants (the defaulting borrower and other named parties with an interest in the premises) to appear in court to defend their positions.

Surplus proceeds Money received by a lender in excess of the unpaid loan balance. In an auction situation, after satisfying the upset price, surplus proceeds from an auction are applied to paying off any other creditors with recorded liens, after which any remaining balance goes to the defaulting borrower.

Survey An illustration of a property description that includes measurements of the structure, improvements, the property area, and the location of boundary lines.

T

Term cap The maximum amount that the interest rate on an adjustable rate loan can go up or down during each adjustment period (usually one-, three-, or five-year anniversary periods).

Terms of sale The contractual obligations of the foreclosure purchaser and the seller.

Title theory states In states that have adopted the title theory, when a property is encumbered with a mortgage or other security device, the lender is the owner of the premises and holds the title and the borrower retains a deed of trust. Title is not passed to the borrower until the borrower pays the loan in full.

Torrens title A recording system used in some states to keep track of all of the legal instruments (liens, deeds, judgments, and so on) associated with a parcel of real property.

Trust deed (deed of trust) A three-party security instrument among the trustor (the borrower), the trustee (an independent title or escrow company), and the beneficiary (the lender) by which title to real property is conveyed to a trustee to hold as security until the trustor pays the loan in full.

Trustee A third party intermediary with no interest in the property, such as a title or escrow company. The trustee holds the title to the property in trust for the benefit of the beneficiary (lender) as security for the debt until the loan is paid in full by the trustor (borrower).

Trustor   When a deed of trust is the security device for a loan, the borrower is the trustor.

U

Underwriter   An individual who works for a lender and has the authority to approve an applicant's loan and issue a commitment on behalf of the lender so that the applicant can purchase a real estate property.

Upset price   The amount set forth in the Judgment of Foreclosure and Sale plus the additional charges (unpaid property taxes, unpaid interest, and so on) that accumulate between the date of the Judgment of Foreclosure and Sale and the date of the auction.

V

Vacancy agreement   An agreement between a tenant and prospective new owner that sets forth the terms under which the tenant will move out of the premises. If all of the conditions in the agreement are met by the tenant, the new owner will pay the tenant a pre-agreed amount of money to relocate to a new dwelling.

W

Waiver of Confidentiality   A statement prepared by the defaulting borrower, usually in a short sale situation, allowing the lender to discuss the borrower's personal loan information directly with a prospective purchaser in an effort to expedite a possible sale before the property is sold at an auction.

Index

About the Author

Melissa Kollen-Rice is a real estate attorney with two decades of experience in the real estate industry.

She began her multifaceted career with a prominent investor group—buying, selling, and creatively financing hundreds of foreclosures. During that time, Melissa obtained her Real Estate Broker's License and Mortgage Broker's License and gained hands-on experience as a property manager and, ultimately, as an investor and a landlord herself.

Melissa's most lucrative transactions involved foreclosed properties, and, drawing on her real life experience and tried and proven techniques, Melissa created seminars to help people purchase foreclosures safely and sanely and performed them for sold-out audiences at colleges and universities. In 1991, McGraw Hill commissioned Melissa to write her first book, entitled, "*Buying Real Estate Foreclosures*," which was updated in 2003.

Melissa has also shared her foreclosure expertise as a guest on radio and television talk shows, including *The Dolans* on CNBC and WOR 710AM; *US News and World Report*; and *Closing Bell* on CNBC. She has been quoted frequently on the topic of foreclosures in *Newsday* and *The New York Times*.

Having grown up in an environment of advocacy all of her life, it was always Melissa's ultimate goal to become an attorney. In 2004, Melissa graduated from Touro Law School and achieved her lifelong dream.

Today, Melissa is an associate attorney at a prominent Long Island, New York law firm, and in addition to assisting clients in purchasing and selling foreclosures and negotiating short sales, Melissa focuses on providing a full range of real estate purchases and sales and rental services for buyers, sellers, landlords, and investors.

Melissa also continues to conduct real estate courses and seminars through L.I. Real Estate Training (LIRET) at many locations in New York. She is a member of the Suffolk County Bar Association, the New York State Bar Association, the Long Island Board of Realtors and the National Association of Realtors.

Write to Melissa at P.O. Box 803, Commack, NY 11725, or contact her via her Web site at LIRET.com.